The Actors Who Could Have Been James Bond

John Fox

Contents

PREFACE

The enduring success of the James Bond franchise has made the casting of a new Bond actor a very big deal in the film and entertainment industry. Tabloids and entertainment clickbait sites love nothing more than constantly speculating (wrongly of course!) on who the next Bond actor might be. Taking on the part of James Bond is like playing the lead in Hamlet, Doctor Who, or Batman. Others have played the part before you and others will play the part after you. Speculation about the next incumbent is therefore inevitable, unavoidable, and endless. It is a constant background hum even when someone else actually has the part.

More people have walked on the moon than played James Bond. Despite the longevity of the franchise the Bond actors themselves remain a small and exclusive club. There are however dozens of actors who might potentially have played James Bond through the decades if only fate hadn't intervened. Michael Billington thought he had the part two or three times in the 70s and 80s but the late return of Roger Moore each time foiled his ambitions. David Warbeck claims that he signed to play James Bond in the early eighties but the film he was supposed to make was abandoned when Roger Moore decided to return as 007. John Gavin DID actually sign to play Bond in Diamonds Are Forever but got the elbow when Sean Connery chose to return. Richard Johnson was offered the part of James Bond in Dr No but declined because he didn't want to be constricted by a long term film contract.

There are many sliding doors moments like this in the Bond franchise where an alternative actor (rather than the one we actually got) could easily have been cast. So how many actors have tested to play James Bond? The answer to that question is an awful lot. When the part of James Bond is being cast it sometimes feels like every actor in Britain and the Commonwealth is up for the part. Literally hundreds of actors have read, auditioned, or simply been interviewed about playing the part of James Bond.

How many of these actors came close to bagging the part? Who might have played Bond if Connery, Lazenby, Moore, Dalton, Brosnan, and Craig hadn't been cast? In the book which follows we will leave no stone unturned and attempt to answer that very question. There is a fascinating alternative cinema universe where the Bond actors are completely different from the ones we ended up with in our own familiar movie dimension. In this book we will explore what that alternative James Bond universe might potentially have looked like.

LONGITUDE 78 WEST & DR NO

The first screen adaptation of James Bond was a 1954 CBS version of Casino Royale as part of Climax Mystery Theater. Barry Nelson portrayed 'Jimmy' Bond - an American card shark. This one hour production obviously wasn't tremendously faithful to Ian Fleming. Bond eventually managed to escape from such curiosities and become a juggernaut movie franchise on the silver screen. The James Bond film franchise (based of course on the popular series of spy thrillers written by Ian Fleming) launched in 1962 is a very special and unique series quite unlike any other. When it began no one could have possibly dreamed of the success and longevity it would enjoy. There had been franchises before Bond - like Tarzan, Sherlock Holmes, Charlie Chan, The Falcon, Jungle Jim, Frankenstein, Lassie, Rin Tin Tin, Bulldog Drummond, Hopalong Cassidy, and many others. As the Bond series began, thrifty but fun franchises like Godzilla and the Carry On films were already becoming popular in their respective countries.

The Bond franchise created by producers Cubby Broccoli and Harry Saltzman however was completely different. Previous film series operated strictly on the law of diminishing returns and lowered the budgets accordingly. They sought to extract every last penny out of their licenced property without actually spending any money. The Bond series reversed this tradition. Each new Bond film was bigger than the one that came before. More lavish, more expensive, more spectacular. It was a gamble that paid off handsomely. Adjusted for inflation, the most successful James Bond film of all time is 1965's Thunderball. Thunderball marked the peak of sixties Bondmania but the series would still go on and on with enduring success and seemingly without end.

In the 1970s a new era of Bond was launched with the unflappable and urbane Roger Moore. Moore went on to make seven films (a record that is unlikely to ever be broken) and proved that the Bond franchise was a perfectly viable ongoing commodity even without Sean Connery. The Bond franchise, with periodic recasting of the lead, could potentially go on forever. James Bond is much bigger than the actor who happens to be playing him. It is a brand as famous as any in cinema. James Bond is completely indestructible. So who else could have played James Bond aside from the six actors we've had at the time of writing? As we shall see, the list of potential Bonds is larger than you might expect.

Although the James Bond franchise was famously established by the producing duo of Cubby Broccoli and Harry Saltzman, they could easily have been beaten to the 007 goldmine by the maverick Irish film producer Kevin McClory. Before the birth of the James Bond movie franchise by Cubby Broccoli and Harry Saltzman, McClory had worked with Ian Fleming on plans for what would have been the first movie featuring James Bond. The screenplay for this proposed Bond film was called Longitude 78 West. Fleming later used Longitude 78 West as the basis for his novel Thunderball. All hell broke loose because Fleming foolishly didn't give McClory or Jack Whittingham (who had also worked on Longitude 78 West) any credit. The inevitable court case which followed left Kevin McClory with the legal right to make a James Bond film based on Thunderball.

Way back in the late 1950s though, McClory was very nearly out of the gate first when it came to deducing the cinematic potential of Ian Fleming's Bond novels. McClory commissioned spectacular art for this proposed new Bond film and the iconography of that art (lavish locations, danger, beautiful women) is indistinguishable from the official Bond imagery of the 1960s. Kevin McClory was confident that Bond could be a big hit on the silver screen and poured all of his ideas and energy into the project. The film was never made in the end but somewhere in an alternative cinema universe now sits a late 1950s Bond film based on an early Thunderball treatment.

It is said that Ian Fleming and the financial backers began to get cold feet about Kevin McClory in the end and suspected he would be out of his depth producing a movie. The project was shelved and Fleming decided (in what was obviously a big mistake) to use the Longitude 78 West treatment as the basis for a new novel he planned to call Thunderball. But who would have played James Bond in this aborted Longitude 78 West film? The number one choice was Richard Burton. Ian Fleming remarked in private correspondence at the time that Burton would make a terrific James Bond and play the part better than anyone. Kevin McClory and Ivar Bryce (a businessman involved in financing the movie) were not inclined to argue. They thought that Burton would be perfect casting too.

At the time Richard Burton was in his mid-thirties and already a star. He had critical acclaim and could more or less pick and choose his projects as he pleased. Though he had read some of Fleming Bond novels and enjoyed them, Burton's interest in 007 did not extend to playing the character in a proposed film. Burton felt that agreeing to appear in a spy adventure caper would be undemanding and pointless at this stage in his career. Burton of course had no way of knowing what an incredibly lucrative phenomenon the Bond films would become. To him, appearing a James Bond film adaptation would just be like making any other film. In this, Burton was completely wrong. Bond films were anything but any other film. They ushered in a new era of cinema and created the modern action adventure movie. James Bond was as big as The Beatles in the 1960s.

Not that Richard Burton had any way of knowing this. Would he even have wanted to do it though, even if he had known how popular the character would be? Burton had no particular desire to be bigger than The Beatles. He would have enough media attention of his own cope with - especially when Elizabeth Taylor entered the super magnified orbit of his life. Besides, there is no way of knowing if James Bond would have been so popular if it had been launched in the 1950s with

Richard Burton. While all the promotional art suggests that Kevin McClory had a good grasp of what a Bond movie should look like there is no way of knowing what sort of film he would have delivered. Would a late 50s Bond film have had the swagger, fun, humour, panache, and lavishness of the Bond series launched by Broccoli and Saltzman only a few years later? It is highly doubtful - at the first attempt anyway.

There is no doubt that Richard Burton would have been a very different Bond to the one played by Sean Connery. Connery deduced that the Bond films were (enjoyably) ludicrous so his James Bond was somewhat tongue-in-cheek. Connery's Bond has his moments of genuine danger and suspense (the train fight with Red Grant for example or laying at the mercy of Goldfinger's laser on that table) but for the most part he's fairly unflappable and having a good time. The biggest difference between the James Bond books written by Ian Fleming and the James Bond film franchise created by Cubby Broccoli and Harry Saltzman was humour. The films gave Bond (played by the peerless and charismatic Connery) deadpan quips and witty lines. Humour became an essential part of the franchise.

Sean Connery and Roger Moore had impeccable timing when it came to dispensing the trademark Bond quips. Richard Burton was unlikely to have approached James Bond in the same spirit. Burton would have played it much straighter and been more of a blood relative to Timothy Dalton and Daniel Craig than Connery and Moore. Not to say that Sean Connery couldn't be tough and dangerous, he obviously could, but his Bond relied on wit and charm as much as his fists or whatever weapons Q branch had supplied. Richard Burton in the late 1950s would have presented a somewhat more plausible and realistic screen version of James Bond. Burton probably would have made it all seem less flippant.

There is certainly no question that Richard Burton would have been very good but would this have been the right Bond at the wrong time? The appeal of the James Bond franchise was that it offered pure fun and escapism. You could forget your troubles for a few hours and be in all of these exotic locations having an adventure with 007. Would the desire of Burton to get more of a grasp on the character and connect it somewhat more to the real world have impinged on the pure fantasy appeal of the movies? Of course, we have no way of knowing how Burton would have played Bond but it's probably safe to assume he wouldn't have done it as a parody or a light hearted tongue firmly in cheek sort of caper.

Despite the gravitas and acting chops of Richard Burton it's hard to see how his Bond could possibly have been as popular than the one played by Sean Connery. That late 1950s version of Thunderball with Burton as James Bond would be a fascinating relic of the era and Bond universe today but would it have kickstarted the James Bond phenomenon in the same way that the early Connery films did? That is simply impossible to say with any degree of certainty but it seems doubtful.

Ian Fleming and Kevin McClory were very interested in Alfred Hitchcock directing their proposed late 1950s Bond film. In many ways, Hitchcock was the perfect person to bring Bond to the screen given his own background in suspense, espionage, and spy adventure thrillers. Fleming and McClory were so keen on acquiring the services of Hitchcock they were even prepared to let Jimmy Stewart play James Bond in the film if this is what it took to hire the legendary Hitch. Thankfully, none of this came to pass. Alfred Hitchcock decided that he did not want to direct a James Bond film and so the unlikely (not to mention eccentric) prospect of James Stewart playing James Bond was never seriously threatened on the general public. It's hard not to think that Stewart as Bond would have been rather like casting Terry Thomas as Indiana Jones. The part was simply all wrong for him. As we shall see though in the pages that follow, Stewart was by no means the last American actor to be linked to the part of James Bond.

Another actor under consideration for the part of James Bond in Kevin McClory's proposed Bond film was Dirk Bogarde. At this time Bogarde was in his late thirties and the most popular film star in Britain. He was best known for the Doctor series of comedy films. Bogarde was not terribly happy in the mainstream though and eager to do different things. He was intent on breaking free from a contract he had at Rank and wanted to play more challenging and daring roles. Bogarde would do all of these things in the 1960s and establish himself as a serious actor. He was fantastic in films like The Servant and Victim.

The main problem that Kevin McClory would have faced casting Dirk Bogarde is probably the fee. Bogarde, because of his immense popularity at the time, would not have been cheap and he wasn't exactly short of work. It is entirely possible that Bogarde would have made the Bond film if his fee had been agreed by all parties but what sort of Bond he would have made is difficult to say. Though he was still boyishly handsome, Bogarde lacked the raw machismo of Sean Connery (or even Richard Burton for that matter) and it's hard to see him playing Bond as a quip machine in the same effortless manner that Connery and Roger Moore did. It's not impossible to see Bogarde having a Timothy Dalton quality to his Bond and playing the agent as more of a quiet thinker.

Another actor that Kevin McClory had on his list of potential Bond actors was his friend Richard Harris. Harris was in his late twenties at the time and had only just begun what would be a long and acclaimed film and television career. A very young Richard Harris playing James Bond is a rather far out and fascinating prospect given the intensity and energy that he brought to his film roles as a young man. Richard Harris didn't really fit the cinematic Bond template soon to be established by Broccoli and Saltzman but there is no doubt that his Bond would have been very compelling. It seems pretty evident though that Harris was not at the top of the list. There were other actors they liked more and - most importantly - were more bankable. This project (had it gone ahead) obviously would have received a considerable boost in profile and publicity with someone of the stature of Richard Burton or the popularity of Dirk Bogarde involved. Richard Harris would not have brought these qualities to the table at the time.

An actor championed by Fleming to be the first James Bond was Peter Finch - an Australian actor who was based in England (where he was born). Finch was in his forties and a prolific film actor. He later won a posthumous Oscar for the 1976 film Network. While he was competent and would have been a safe pair of hands it's hard to see how a Peter Finch Bond would have set the pulses racing in the same manner that Sean Connery's did or Richard Burton might have. Fleming was also allegedly amenable to the idea of Trevor Howard playing James Bond. While there is no question that Howard was a great figure of cinema and a fine actor, he doesn't seem like a very daring choice to play Bond. Fleming seemed to concede in private notes that Howard might be a little too mature and austere to bring 007 to life. Howard felt like someone who should be playing M rather than Bond.

The actor Terence Cooper was also in contention to play Bond in McClory's film. Cooper later played one of the many James Bonds in the 1967 spoof Casino Royale. He later played a number of parts in Australia and New Zealand. Cooper was tall and dark-haired and looked fairly Bondish in Casino Royale. He wouldn't have been a bad shout for the part. Kevin McClory is later said to have later approached Laurence Harvey to play James Bond in his planned 1960s version of Thunderball (which obviously didn't go ahead). Laurence Harvey was a Lithuanian-born English actor in his early thirties. He had appeared in films like Room at the Top and The Manchurian Candidate. Harvey was a stylish looking man who was handsome in a slightly cruel sort of way. He could be both charming and caddish - which would appear to be two very 007 qualities. The one doubt about Laurence Harvey is whether he could have been believably tough as 007 because he was a rather emaciated looking man. One suspects he would have needed to put on some weight to be a credible Bond.

Cubby Broccoli was very shrewd in the way that he handled Kevin McClory. He brought McClory in as a co-producer on EON's 1965 film version of Thunderball and made McClory agree not to produce a Thunderball film of his own for at least ten years. Broccoli probably presumed (not unreasonably) the James Bond series wouldn't even be around in ten years time. Once the ten years were up though, the Bond series was still around and Kevin McClory set about making his own Bond film. McClory's plans to make a Bond film in the seventies called Warhead were frustrated but his long threatened unofficial renegade Bond film finally arrived in 1983 with Never Say Never Again.

When the proposed late fifties Bond film was abandoned (eventually to descend into bitter legal battles in court), this paved the way for others to bring James Bond to the big screen. The James Bond books were turned into a movie franchise in 1962 by New York born film producer Albert 'Cubby' Broccoli and Canadian producer Harry Saltzman. Before he became a film producer, Cubby Broccoli had a spell selling coffins. He was also a Christmas tree salesman at one point. Dr No was eventually chosen to be the first film adaptation.

"Harry Saltzman held the option on Ian Fleming's James Bond stories," said Broccoli, "and I offered him a partnership. He considered them a bit of nonsense. I thought they offered all the basics in screen entertainment: a virile and resourceful hero, exotic locations, the ingenious apparatus of espionage and sex on a sophisticated level. It's true they had been around for a long time, and none of the leading British and American producers had made a serious pitch for them." Cubby Broccoli used to be a business partner with the famous American producer Irwin Allen. When Cubby told Allen he wanted to option the Bond books, Allen told him the Fleming novels were awful and wouldn't even be worthy of television. He was obviously completely wrong about that.

Ian Fleming's James Bond books were very popular because their blend of sex, sadism, and dangerous adventure felt like something new and even risque at the time. British readers loved the James Bond books in the 1950s because the exotic nature of the novels was an escape from the lingering post-war austerity they still experienced. Fleming once wrote that the James Bond books were written for 'for warm-blooded heterosexuals in railway trains, airplanes and beds'. Bond's code number '007' was apparently inspired by a bus route in Kent which was often taken by the author Ian Fleming. The literary Bond suffers from "accidie" - this is Fleming's definition of boredom and the deadliest of all sins for James Bond. The profile of the Bond novels got a huge boost when President John F. Kennedy named From Russia With Love as one of his books of the year.

As part of the deal with Ian Fleming to bring James Bond to the big screen, it was agreed that EON (the company created by Broccoli and Saltzman to produce the movies - EON means Everything or Nothing) would have permission to write original Bond films if they exhausted the Fleming stories. This was obviously a shrewd agreement on the part of the film producers. When the Bond movie franchise began, Ian Fleming was allowed to sit in on production meetings and had final script approval.

The James Bond movie franchise tended to cherrypick titles, character names, and scenes from the Fleming books rather than adapt them wholesale. To give an example, the 1979 film Moonraker has little to do with Ian Fleming's 1955 novel of the same name - aside from the villain having the name Hugo Drax. The movie is about a villain who wants to create a new utopia in space whereas the book is about a secret government missile project on the Kent coast that James Bond has to investigate. Bond films tended not to be very faithful to the books at all. When they were actually more faithful (see On Her Majesty's Secret Service as the most example) the artistic results were plain to see.

Broccoli and Saltzman had finally managed to put in a deal in place for the first Bond movie to be produced but now they had the not inconsiderable task of finding the right actor to play Bond. This would be their first experience of what you might describe as the 007 casting circus. The casting of a new Bond involves hundreds of interviews, readings, auditions, and screen tests. There is no particular science about it. The process simply has to find an actor who everyone (the producers and the studio) can agree upon. The lack of a specific criteria for what sort of person they wanted was evident in the eclectic sweep of the Dr No casting calls. Mature and famous actors were approached to play James Bond in Dr No but so were inexperienced unknown young actors too. No one really seemed to have a firm idea of who they wanted.

When the first James Bond film was being planned, Ian Fleming sent Broccoli and Saltzman a memo with his own thoughts about the approach they should take. 'Atmosphere: To my mind, the greatest danger in this series is too much stage Englishness,' wrote Fleming. 'There should, I think, be no monocles, moustaches, bowler hats or bobbies or other "Limey" gimmicks. There should be no blatant English slang, a minimum of public school ties and accents.' Fleming wanted the Bond films to feel modern and bold. Broccoli and Saltzman shared this vision. Cubby Broccoli's own take was that Bond films should be set 'five minutes into the future'. They should exist in a world that is more or less our own but heightened slightly.

It is often said that Ian Fleming wanted Roger Moore to play James Bond in Dr No but any evidence for this is hard to verify. Moore said that he wasn't approached for Dr No at all - although Cubby Broccoli wrote in his memoir that Roger was a person they briefly discussed in casting discussions but then dismissed because they felt he still looked too boyish and callow. At the time Roger Moore was in his early thirties and on the lower rung of the studio system in Hollywood. Roger's attempt to become a star in the United States, despite frequent work, did not gain much traction and he eventually returned to

England to play Simon Templar on television - thus setting him on a 'long way around' path to James Bond in the future.

One name at the top of the list for 007 was the Northern Ireland born Hollywood actor Stephen Boyd. Boyd was about thirty years-old and had appeared in films like Ben Hur and The Bravados. Boyd was handsome, urbane, cool, and had a fantastic deep voice. In fact, there was a Connery-esque quality about Boyd. You easily picture him playing James Bond in the 1960s. Alas though, Boyd was not interested in the part and declined the invitation to be considered for Dr No. He later appeared in films like Fantastic Voyage and Shalako (with Sean Connery). Sadly, Stephen Boyd died far too young in 1977.

The James Bond series did invent the big budget action franchise but even Cubby Broccoli and Harry Saltzman had their own influences. The Bond series was heavily influenced by Alfred Hitchcock's masterful 1959 suspense thriller North By Northwest. North By Northwest was in many ways the first James Bond film. It has a suave leading man, adventure, action, varied locations, panache, urbane villains, suggestive humour. The helicopter sequence in From Russia With Love is clearly inspired the cropdusting sequence in North By Northwest. The Bond producers were so inspired by North By Northwest that they even tried to persuade Cary Grant (who was a friend of Cubby Broccoli) to play James Bond in Dr No. Grant, who was in his early sixties at the time, wisely declined this offer though because he felt he was far too old for the part and wanted to retire from acting anyway.

The search for Dr No's James Bond actor relieved an awful lot of publicity in the British newspapers and the Daily Express even ran a competition to find the perfect Bond. A number of male model types and aspiring actors were run through their paces and the winner was judged to be a twenty-eight year-old model named Peter Anthony. Anthony's photographs were passed onto Broccoli and Saltzman and he was invited to do an official test. Nothing came of this (though he looked terrific it was obviously Anthony's acting inexperience which provided the biggest obstacle to his James Bond dream) but Anthony was invited to test again for Diamonds Are Forever nearly a decade later so Broccoli and Saltzman must have liked him.

The other finalists in the Express competition were salesmen Gordon Cooper and Anthony Clements, a former teacher named Frank Ellement, and an engineer named Michael Ricketts. Another finalist was a stuntman named Bob Simmons. Simmons would (in a fashion) become the first Bond because it is him and not Sean Connery we see in the gunbarrel intro for Dr No. It was reported in the media in 1961 that Broccoli and Saltzman were having a rather difficult time trying to find their James Bond for Dr No and had the pushed production back to give them time to conduct a more thorough search. None of the famous names they approached seemed terribly keen and there was still a sense that they didn't know quite what they were looking for. Some of the actors they tested were very young but they still hadn't ruled out casting someone more mature and famous. The net was being cast very deep and wide in the hope that the right person might magically emerge and suddenly win everyone around.

The producers were quite keen on Patrick McGoohan as a James Bond candidate for Dr No. McGoohan was well known at the time for playing John Drake in the television series Danger Man. McGoohan was not only a competent actor but also a proven leading man (albeit on the small screen rather than cinema) who brought an enjoyably offbeat wit to his parts. Broccoli and Saltzman were disappointed to learn though that Patrick McGoohan had no interest in playing James Bond and considered Bond to be morally dubious. "It has an insidious and powerful influence on children," said McGoohan when asked why he had turned down the chance to be James Bond in Dr No. "Would you like your son to grow up like James Bond? Since I hold these views strongly as an individual and parent I didn't see how I could contribute to the very things to which I objected." McGoohan would later become best known for creating and starring in the surreal television classic The Prisoner.

As the search rumbled on, Ian Fleming continued to float names which were not terribly realistic or very forward thinking. Fleming suggested that Trevor Howard (again) or Stewart Granger might make a good Bond but both of these names were more of past bygone eras than a modern new franchise for the Swinging Sixties. This was equally the case with Edward Underdown - who Fleming also suggested. Most of the names that Fleming proposed were simply too old for the part (which does tend to suggest that Fleming saw James Bond as a mature sort of character). The handsome if slightly sinister looking Undertown, who later had a small part in Thunderball and was a prolific film actor, was in his fifties and nearly thirty years older than some of the young actors they were looking at. Undertown clearly wasn't a great candidate on the grounds of age alone.

Another person who is sometimes linked to the part of Bond in Dr No is Michael Redgrave. Although a fine actor, Redgrave was already in his fifties and so would have also been a pretty pointless person to pursue on the grounds of age alone. What the producers needed was an actor capable of making sequels (if the film was successful enough to earn sequels that is) and Redgrave wasn't that person. Rex Harrison is another actor said to have been suggested by Fleming but this is difficult to verify. Harrison, like Redgrave, was simply too old to be a serious candidate. There wouldn't be much point in hiring an actor as a one-off. EON definitely needed to start thinking about younger actors.

Another mature actor who was courted to play Bond in Dr No was James Mason. Mason was offered a three film contract but declined the offer because he didn't want to be contracted to a series of spy caper films. James Mason was in his fifties and although suave and a terrific actor he was already far too old for the part. Equally unrealistic from an age point of view was David Niven - who Fleming continued to suggest. One can only presume that some of these names were floated on the grounds that the producers and Fleming thought it might be easier to sell the film with an established and well known actor attached. Deep down though they must have known that what they really needed was an exciting young actor who came with no baggage and therefore would be accepted by audiences as 007 straight away.

Another of Fleming's suggestions was Richard Todd. Todd was in his early forties at the time so slightly more realistic in terms of age than some of the other candidates. He was known for films like The Dam Busters and The Hasty Heart and a very old-fashioned type of leading man. Despite his ability to play stiff upper lipped war heroes, it's hard to see how a Richard Todd version of James Bond would have launched the series into the stratosphere in the manner that Sean Connery did. Todd just seemed too old fashioned for sixties Bond mania. It all became academic in the end anyway as Richard Todd could not be considered for Dr No due to scheduling commitments on other films. He was simply too busy to throw his hat into the Bond casting circus.

A very plausible candidate was the beefy Australian actor Rod Taylor. Taylor was in his early thirties at the time of Dr No and was handsome (in a dated 1960s male model type of way) and likeable. He had just made The Time Machine and was soon to feature in The Birds for Alfred Hitchcock. He had a television show called Hong Kong at the time of Dr No - which was an attempt to turn Taylor into a big star. Taylor was approached about becoming the first ever big screen James Bond but he rebuffed the interest. This was something he soon came to regret. "I refused because I thought it was beneath me," said Taylor. "I didn't think Bond would be successful in the movies. That was one of the greatest mistakes of my career! Every time a new Bond picture became a smash hit, I tore out my hair!" For whatever reason Rod Taylor never really became a big star in the end. That obviously wouldn't have been the case if he'd done James Bond. For a taste of what a Rod Taylor Bond might have been like, watch the 1965 film The Liquidator - in which Taylor plays the spy "Boysie" Oakes.

Another actor who was considered to play Bond in Dr No was Patrick Allen. Allen was in his mid-thirties and had appeared in many films - including Dunkirk and I Was Monty's Double. Allen would later become better known as a voice over artist and announcer on Channel 4 but he continued to act right through to the nineties. Allen would later take on a James Bondish sort of role when he played a military investigator trying to solve an alien mystery in the daft 1969 sci-fi adventure film The Body Stealers. Despite his fame as a comedic continuity man, Allen was a perfectly decent (not to mention prolific) actor in his younger years. Though lantern jawed and quite good looking in an old-fashioned sort of way it is debatable if Allen had the right look for Bond.

An actor on the radar of the producers was 32 year-old Michael Craig. Craig was tall and handsome and a prolific British film actor. He did not though go on to become a very big star (Craig eventually moved to Australia and mostly worked there). The main reason for this is that Craig didn't have much range as an actor. Michael Craig was one of those actors who just seemed to give the same performance in everything - no matter who he was portraying. Exploitation buffs might recognise Michael Craig as the evil commandant in the cultishly gruesome 1982 film Turkey Shoot. Though the producers had Patrick Allen and Craig on their long list of Bond candidates it doesn't appear that either of them got very far in the process or were ever extensively auditioned. Michael Craig would have looked the part but whether he would have been a very exciting or charismatic 007 is open to question.

James Fox was considered to play Bond in Dr No according to Cubby Broccoli in his memoir. Fox was in his early twenties at the time and had appeared in The Loneliness of the Long Distance Runner. He was about to make the brilliant drama film The Servant with Dirk Bogarde. Fox, given his youth, would have been bold casting but according to Cubby Broccoli he did not want to play the part and displayed no interest in becoming a candidate. Edward Fox, the brother of James, later played M in Never Say Never Again. Ian Hendry was another actor who appeared on a long list of potential Bond candidates for Dr No. Hendry was best known for appearing in the first series of The Avengers. Though a terrific actor, Hendry didn't really look the part and definitely would have needed a toupee. Hendry's career was blighted by alcoholism but he still managed to clock up some cultish roles in the 1970s through films like Theatre of Blood, Tales from the Crypt, and Damien: Omen II.

William Franklyn was another actor of the era who was interviewed about playing Bond in Dr No. Franklyn, rather like Patrick Allen, would became more famous as a pitchman than an actor. Franklyn fronted the "Schhh... You Know Who" adverts for Schweppes from 1965 to 1973. He was in his mid-thirties around the time of Dr No and although the right sort of age it doesn't appear that William Franklyn got very far in the Bond casting calls. You may have seen Franklyn in British films like Quatermass 2, The Satanic Rites of Dracula, and The Intelligence Men (with Eric Morecambe and Ernie Wise). Though a crisp and competent actor Franklyn probably didn't have the right look for 007.

Another actor who was on a list of Dr No Bond candidates was George Baker. Baker was about thirty years-old at the time and had appeared in films like The Dam Busters. In the end Baker could not be considered for Dr No because he was contracted to another film. Baker later had parts in On Her Majesty's Secret Service and The Spy Who Loved Me in addition to an uncredited role in You Only Live Twice. His many television roles included I, Cladius and The Ruth Rendell Mysteries. Though a very good actor, it's hard to see George Baker playing James Bond in Dr No.

The widow of the great Welsh actor Stanley Baker claimed that he was offered a three film contract to play James Bond - beginning of course with Dr No. Baker was on the cusp of becoming a star at the time and a few years later would take the lead role in the classic historical war film Zulu. Baker, according to his widow, did not want to be tied to a long term contract and so declined the offer. He is later said to have regretted this decision (especially when his career hit the buffers and he suffered from financial trouble) but Baker did later say that he thought Sean Connery was the perfect choice for the role. Stanley Baker certainly had the stature and talent to play Bond but would have been unlikely to bring the wit and playfulness that Connery so memorably brought to the role.

The swords-and-sandals star, bodybuilder, and actor Steve Reeves said that he turned down an approach to play Bond in Dr No because the offer was $100,000 and he was already making more than double that on his Hercules pictures in Italy. Reeves was a handsome fellow but whether he had the acting chops to play Bond is another matter. And would you really want James Bond to have the body of Arnold Schwarzenegger? It doesn't quite seem right somehow for Bond to look like a bodybuilder. Another unlikely candidate was the American film director John Frankenheimer. Frankenheimer claimed that as a young man he was offered the chance to audition for the part of Bond in Dr No. "I was offered the role of James Bond in 1962. I was at a nightclub in London, and (Bond producer) Cubby Broccoli saw me. And I looked just like what Ian Fleming had written, and he asked me would I do it? And I turned him down."

The problems of finding a Bond actor were nearly matched by the trouble finding a director on Dr No. Guy Hamilton, Guy Green, Ken Hughes, and Bryan Forbes all turned down an offer to direct the first Bond film. This opened the door for Terence Young. Young was an experienced and competent director but more importantly than that he was also rather like a real life James Bond. Young was urbane and sophisticated and enjoyed the finer things in life. He was an expert on fashion and food. Young took on an active role in the search for Bond when he was hired as he was quite dismayed by some of the candidates he was viewing. He decided he would simply find his own candidate.

The man that Terence Young chose to play James Bond was 34 year-old Richard Johnson. Johnson was from the Royal Shakespeare Company and at the beginning of his film career. Johnson was urbane, handsome, dark-haired, and seemed like a pretty good selection. Young urged the producers to sign Johnson and so, in light of the fact that none of the other candidates had exactly blown their socks off, Broccoli and Saltzman offered Johnson a three film contract. At this though Johnson recoiled. "The producers, Albert Broccoli and Harry Saltzman, asked me - at Terence Young's instigation - and I turned the job down," said Johnson. "I was under contract to MGM anyway, so that gave me a reasonable excuse to say no, because they told me I'd have to be under exclusive contract to them for seven years. Eventually they offered it to Sean Connery, who was completely wrong for the part. But in getting the wrong man they got the right man, because it turned the thing on its head and he made it funny. And that's what propelled it to success."

Richard Johnson was definitely the one that got away when it came to Dr No. The part was his for the asking but he simply didn't want to do it. One thing we have to factor in is that in 1961 no one had any idea if a Bond film would be a big deal or not. The books were popular but that was no guarantee that a Bond feature film would be a success. Richard Johnson, like all of the actors approached for Dr No, had no idea that the James Bond films were going to be the pop culture phenomenon of the 1960s and make vast quantities of money. But how much of a factor was Sean Connery in this? As Terence Young once said - "If you asked me what were the three ingredients for James Bond, it was Sean Connery, Sean Connery and Sean Connery!"

As with the other potential first 007 candidates, it is impossible to see how a Richard Johnson version of James Bond would have been anywhere near as exciting or funny as the one played by Sean Connery. Connery set such a high bar that even people who DIDN'T get the part suffered in comparison. It's hard to know if Richard Johnson ever regretted turning down James Bond but he later appeared in a number of forgettable Bond inspired spy capers (Deadlier Than the Male, Some Girls Do, Danger Route) in the 1960s. The irony of this surely couldn't have been lost on Johnson. Johnson eventually enjoyed a very long and eclectic career. His film roles included The Haunting, Zombi 2, Lara Croft: Tomb Raider, and The Boy in the Striped Pyjamas.

The problems in casting James Bond felt like divine intervention in the end because it paved the way for the right candidate to finally emerge. That candidate was a 30 year-old Scottish actor named Sean Connery. Connery had been an artist's model, body builder, and coffin polisher before he took up acting. It was apparently the 1959 Disney film Darby O'Gill and the Little People which put Connery on the EON radar. Cubby Broccoli's wife Dana saw Connery in this film and told her husband that Connery was sexy. When the producers met Sean Connery they were impressed by the macho magnetism he seemed to project.

'One face kept coming back into my mind,' wrote Cubby Broccoli in his memoir. 'He was Sean Connery, a tall, personable man, projecting a kind of animal virility and just the right hint of threat behind that hard smile. I was convinced he was the closest we could get to Fleming's super-hero. We sent footage to United Artists in New York, who'd put up the $1 million. They sent back a telegram: 'NO – KEEP TRYING.' We wired back, insisting that Connery was the man we wanted and we weren't searching any further.'

Connery was scruffy and laid-back when he met the producers. He wasn't someone to put on heirs and graces. "I had first met Sean in Cubby's office back at the beginning," said Moneypenny actress Lois Maxwell. "He had that wonderful atmosphere of menace and moved, as Cubby said, like a panther. But he was still a poor young actor in rumpled corduroys who looked like he lived in a bedsit." Connery was even reluctant to do a test for Bond. He said the producers simply decide if they wanted him or not on the strength of his other work (which was limited at the time as Connery had only been acting for several years).

Terence Young hated the choice of Sean Connery at first ("Disaster!" Young is said to have declared when he heard Connery was cast) but quickly realised that Connery could be very good if he was cleaned up somewhat. Terence Young played a big role in the transformation of Connery. Young had his tailor cut sharp suits for Connery and taught him how to be more elegant and refined onscreen. Young got Sean Connery a Saville Row suit for Dr No and told him to sleep in it! Young wanted Connery to feel like an expensive suit was like a second skin. The friendship between Terence Young and Sean Connery on the early Bond films is said to have mitigated the fact that Connery didn't like the Bond producers very much. When he was cast as James Bond, Connery worked with a dance teacher named Yat Malmgren so he could learn how to be more graceful and panther like in his movements and gestures.

Ian Fleming also initially hated the choice of Sean Connery to play James Bond. Fleming thought that Connery was too rough and not refined enough to play his hero. He even compared him to a truck driver. However, Fleming changed his mind when he saw Connery in action. He thought Connery was fantastic. Ian Fleming lived long enough to see Dr No and From Russia With Love made into movies but - sadly - he died just before the release of Goldfinger. Fleming therefore never quite got to experience the peak Bondmania that his famous character created in the 1960s with Goldfinger and Thunderball. Peter Hunt, the editor on the early Bond films, said they only realised what a sensation they had on their hands when they screened Dr No for an audience. Before that, they genuinely didn't know if audiences would like Dr No or not.

Sean Connery said he enjoyed making the first few Bond films but it became a drag in the end. "The first two or three were fun. The cast made it fun. Jumping out of planes was entertaining although it was tough on my hair piece. It eventually became too dominant in everything I was doing. There was no way to compete with it and try to get any justifiable balance." The Bond films soon got bigger and bigger as the money rolled in. Thunderball was so popular in Britain that some cinemas sold all their seats and then sold extra tickets to customers who were willing to stand! Demand for Thunderball was so great that they had two simultaneous premieres in London full of celebrities, glitz, and huge crowds of fans. Sean Connery never turned up to either of them.

All of the later James Bond actors have had to stand in the shadow cast by the Sean Connery. George Lazenby once said that the post-Connery Bonds were essentially all imposters trying to play a role that belonged to Sean. Connery had screen presence, charisma, perfect timing, machismo, acting ability, and wit. He was the complete package. None of the other Bond actors (whatever their individual strengths) were quite able to tick every box in the way that Sean Connery did (and with considerable ease too). Connery's Bond could be cruel and ruthless but he was also charming and funny. No other Bond actor was able to project an irresistible blend of power and panache in the fashion that Connery could. Connery's Bond was dangerous but he was also fun. That was the perfect template for the cinematic version of Ian Fleming's character.

Sean Connery has to take a generous portion of the credit for the Bond films becoming such a phenomenon that they still exist today. The 60s Bonds were the foundation upon which an apparently indestructible film franchise was built. Dr No made nearly $60 million from a budget of only one million and the profits on the following films would be even more spectacular. Goldfinger was so popular that its soundtrack knocked the Beatles off the top of the American albums chart. Production began on Goldfinger before From Russia with Love had even been released to cinemas. The producers were super confident (even at this early stage) that they had a winning formula.

The late film critic Roger Ebert felt that Goldfinger was the movie which established the Bond formula. 'The Broccoli-Saltzman formula found its lasting form in the making of "Goldfinger." The outline was emerging in the first two films, and here it is complete. First, the title sequence, establishing Bond as a sex hound while linking him with a stunt sequence or a spectacular death. Then the summons by M, head of British Secret Service, and the briefing on a villain obsessed by global domination. The flirtation with Moneypenny. The demonstration by Q of new gimmicks invented especially for his next case. Then the introduction of the villain, his murderous and bizarre sidekick, and his female assistant/accomplice/mistress. Bond's discovery of the nature of the villain's evil scheme. Bond's capture and the certainty of death. Bond's seduction of the villain's woman. And so on, leading always to a final scene in which Bond is about to enjoy his victory reward: the sensuous fruits of his latest conquest.' Cubby Broccoli felt however that From Russia with Love was the movie which set in stone the Bond template.

Sean Connery said that no one had the faintest idea if Dr No was going to become a success when they were making it. "Everyone who said that the first one was going to be a success is a liar because they didn't know. The film costs less than a million dollars. They didn't make one immediately afterwards because they still weren't sure. Everybody forgets that. Believe me, nobody could have foreseen that all these years later, we'd be sitting here discussing James Bond." The weather in Jamaica was quite bad when they made Dr No and they couldn't shoot half the scenes they'd planned. United Artists had threatened to pull the plug on Dr No when the film overan its production budget. It's a good job they didn't. The entire course of cinematic history might have been altered!

Sean Connery would make five Bond films in the 1960s. It was as if the union of this actor and this character was always destined to happen. You couldn't really imagine anyone else playing the sixties Bond. Connery was perfect. Though the role catapulted Connery to the A'list it did not bring him artistic happiness. Sean Connery quickly tired of the fame and attention afforded to him by Bondmania in the 1960s. Connery called James Bond his Frankenstein's Monster. In the period between Thunderball and You Only Live Twice, Connery did an interview in which he said - "The Bond pictures have become like comic strips dependent on bigger and better gimmicks. That's all that sustains them. There are even dolls with spikes that protrude from their shoes. It's a lot of rubbish."

One of the main reasons why Connery left the franchise was that he felt it was constrictive playing the same character all the time. He wanted to embrace new challenges as an actor and get away from his Bond image. Connery was frustrated that the Bond films became increasingly elaborate and lengthy productions because this made it more difficult for him to find the time to play other more rewarding (from his point of view) roles. There are other reasons too why Sean Connery tired of playing James Bond. For one, he felt like he had no privacy anymore. Wherever he went he was besieged by fans. Connery couldn't even go out for a quiet meal without being asked for an autograph (his annoyance was frequently made worse by people asking him to sign autographs 'James Bond' rather than Sean Connery). Around the time that Thunderball was released, Sean Connery received about 1,500 fan letters a week.

Another reason why Connery became embittered was money. Broccoli and Saltzman were raking it in with the Bond franchise in the 1960s and Connery felt he should have been made a partner and given a more generous share of the profits. "It's not that I needed the money," said Connery in 1971, "I'm a relatively wealthy man. It was the fact that I put in an awful lot of work and energy into the Bond pictures and was not sufficiently rewarded. The producers were getting greedy. I had an awful time getting the money out of them."

In mitigation, Broccoli and Saltzman might have argued that they were the ones who made Connery a film star in the first place. Sean Connery would have been nowhere near as rich and famous without James Bond.

Were Connery's complaints about money justified? The evidence suggests he had a case. Even adjusted for inflation, Sean Connery is the lowest paid Bond actor after George Lazenby. In today's money, Connery earned about $3.5 million per Bond film. By way of contrast, Daniel Craig was paid an average of around $10 million per Bond film. Roger Moore was paid double Sean's salary on his Bond films. You can certainly argue a strong case that Cubby and Harry should have given Connery a more generous share of the profits. In his career after James Bond, it is claimed that Sean Connery was very forensic when it came to profit share deals on movies and even hired accountants for the specific task of investigating the profits of each film he made to make sure he wasn't being short-changed. This was no doubt a reaction to his sense that Broccoli and Saltzman had short-changed him on the Bond films.

In 1967, Sean Connery's brother Neil starred in an Italian James Bond knock-off film called O.K. Connery (aka Operation Kid Brother). A large number of familiar faces from the Bond films appeared in the movie with Neil Connery - including Bernard Lee, Lois Maxwell, Adolfo Celi, and Daniela Bianchi. Neil Connery looked a little bit like Sean but had none of his brother's charisma or screen presence. Neil was dubbed in the film because he had a medical condition involving his throat at the time and couldn't speak very well. O.K. Connery is terrible film objectively but could be seen as a guilty pleasure. Lois Maxwell said that Sean Connery was very angry that Bond regulars had agreed to appear in the Italian movie and felt betrayed by them. The ironic thing is that Lois Maxwell was better paid on O.K. Connery than she ever was on the Bond movies!

The absolute apex of Sean Connery's annoyance with all things 007 is said to have famously arrived when a photographer tried to follow him into the toilet and take his picture while he was shooting You Only Live Twice. That was the final straw.

Connery declined to return after this film was completed. At the time there had been plans to make On her Majesty's Secret Service with Connery but a new leading man would be required now. vice was originally supposed to follow Thunderball in the film series. At one point, Sean Connery was actually under contract to appear in On Her Majesty's Secret Service.

Finding a James Bond actor in 1961 had been difficult enough but now the producers faced what appeared to be an impossible task. They had to somehow find an actor capable of replacing Sean Connery. The Bond posters of the 1960s were always emblazoned with the legend Sean Connery IS James Bond. That was the problem. Sean Connery was the perfect Bond and the only Bond. Who would be foolish enough to want to replace him?

ON HER MAJESTY'S SECRET SERVICE

Before the drama of casting 007 in On Her Majesty's Secret Service began, Roger Moore had a vague approach to play James Bond in the late 1960s. Cubby and Harry were thinking about making The Man with the Golden Gun at the time and thought Roger (now popular and famous thanks to the television show The Saint) might be a safe pair of hands for the franchise. Roger was a neighbour of Harry Saltzman in the 1960s and knew both Cubby and Harry quite well. "At that time they were talking about going to Cambodia," said Roger, "and all hell broke loose and things got postponed. Lew Grade decided to sell a series Tony Curtis and I were doing - The Persuaders - which sort of precluded me from doing Bond. Then they had the search and came up with George Lazenby."

One actor who was invited to a Bond casting call for On Her Majesty's Secret Service was a certain Timothy Dalton. Dalton had just appeared in the film The Lion in Winter. However, Dalton felt that at twenty-four he was far too young to even consider playing James Bond. Though invited to a OHMSS casting call, Dalton didn't even bother to turn up. More than anything it was the thought of having to replace the seemingly irreplaceable Sean Connery that made Dalton spurn any chance (however remote - he was simply invited to a casting call and never offered the part) to throw his hat into the ring. "When Sean Connery gave up the role," said Dalton, "I guess I, alongside quite a few other actors, was approached about the possibility of playing the part. That was for OHMSS. I was very flattered, but I think anybody would have been off their head to have taken over from Connery. I was also too young. Bond should be a man in his mid-30s, at least - a mature adult who has been around."

Terence Stamp, a hip young actor at the time thanks to films like Far from the Madding Crowd and Modesty Blaise, was taken out to dinner by Harry Saltzman in 1968 to discuss becoming the new James Bond but Stamp seemed very self-conscious about replacing Sean Connery and didn't make a great impression on Harry. "I was taken out to dinner by Harry Saltzman," said Stamp, "and he put it out there that he'd be interested in me doing it. I was flattered, but felt so self-conscious because Sean had been so successful, so identified with it. I said to Harry: 'Let's do the one where Bond is disguised as a Japanese. I'd play the whole film in the disguised make-up and at the very end, you see it's me!' I thought this very unusual idea would get over the self-consciousness of there suddenly being a different 007. I think my ideas about it put the frighteners on Harry. I didn't get a second call from him. Like most English actors, I'd have loved to be 007 because I really know how to wear a suit."

Though it might seem like a rather offbeat idea at first glance, Cubby Broccoli said that they seriously considered Oliver Reed as Sean Connery's replacement. Reed was someone who had the intensity and screen presence to make an interesting Bond but whether he looked the part (Oliver Reed was definitely a bulky sort of chap and this always made him look like he was carrying too much weight) is another matter altogether.

"Oliver Reed was very near the top of the list," said Cubby Broccoli. "Lazenby was an unknown. We could mould Lazenby into the public perception of James Bond, into the kind of Bond we knew the fans wanted. With Oliver Reed we would have had a far greater problem. Oliver already had a public image; he was well known and working hard at making himself even better known. We would have had to destroy that image and rebuild Oliver Reed as James Bond – and we just didn't have the time or the money."

Oliver Reed was about thirty years-old around the time that On Her Majesty's Secret Service was being cast. The year that OHMSS came out, Reed starred with Diana Rigg and Telly Savalas in the black comedy The Assassination Bureau. Rigg and Savalas would of course be cast in OHMSS. One obvious factor that might have gone against Oliver Reed becoming James Bond is his notorious status as a boozy hellraiser and prankster. You can't really picture Oliver Reed as the most sensible brand ambassador for the Bond franchise!

Oliver Reed was riding very high in the late sixties thanks to films like Oliver! and Women in Love. Artistically he didn't really need James Bond but he probably would have found it hard to turn down the money if an offer had been made.

Although it is sometimes reported that Michael Caine turned down the part of Bond after Connery left there doesn't seem to be any firm evidence for this. Caine was certainly one of the most famous actors in Britain at the time but he was far more suited to the Harry Palmer films (produced by Harry Saltzman) where he played a world weary sarcastic working-class spy who was a million miles away from 007. Michael Caine has said he would have turned down Bond for fear of being typecast but it seems that no one actually stepped forward to offer him the part anyway. One thing that might have put Caine off Bond is hearing his friend Sean Connery constantly complain about the producers and the franchise. It's not as if Caine was short of money or parts. He would continue to be one of the busiest film actors in the world for decades to come.

The American actor Roy Thinnes was briefly sized up as a potential new Bond when he was in London shooting the Gerry Anderson film Doppelgänger. Thinnes was in his early thirties and had just finished his stint as the lead in the short lived sci-fi show The Invaders. Thinnes, who would have been the first blond Bond had he been cast!, did not become a serious contender for the part of 007 in OHMSS though. The boss of United Artists, David Picker, had an eccentric idea concerning the new Bond. Picker suggested that they cast the popular tennis ace John Newcombe as Bond. He thought it would be a great story to have this good looking sporting hero become a film star. Picker's idea predictably didn't stand up to much scrutiny and in the end no one was crazy enough to hand a tennis player the most famous acting gig in the world.

Another far-fetched candidate was Peter Purves. Purves played Steven Taylor in Doctor Who and would soon become famous as one of the presenters on Blue Peter. Purvis said that he was invited to audition for the part of Bond in OHMSS but he was never likely to get very far in the audition process. An even more eccentric candidate than Purvis was

Richard John Bingham (7th Earl of Lucan) - commonly known as Lord Lucan. Lucan was in his mid-thirties and quite dashing in an old-fashioned aristocratic sort of way. He even owned an Aston Martin. Lucan haunted the gentlemen's clubs of London so knew the Bond producers and had known the late Ian Fleming too. He was invited to do a test for OHMSS but decided not to accept the offer. The story goes that Lucan had previously done a disastrous test for a Peter Sellers film called Woman Times Seven and decided that acting definitely wasn't for him.

Several years later, Lucan would become the most famous missing person in Britain thanks to a puzzling murder mystery. In November 1974, his wife Veronica and nanny Sandra Rivett were attacked in their home. Rivett was killed while Veronica survived and said that her husband had been the one who attacked them. Lucan was obviously the prime suspect in this case but he completely vanished and was never seen again. No one knows what happened to him. It seems plausible that Lucan might have taken his own life after the double murder attempt but the truth is that we simply don't know.

Another (what you might describe as) frivolous candidate for OHMSS was Peter Snow. Snow claims that he was invited to test for OHMSS. He would become best known as a political journalist and was a fixture on the BBC's Election night coverage for many years. Even in his younger photographs, Snow looks nothing like James Bond. Peter Snow said it best when he remarked that he would have been more suited to playing Q than Bond. An equally silly rumoured candidate was Dick Van Dyke - who claimed that Cubby Broccoli asked him to test in the late 1960s. Van Dyke reminded Broccoli that he was famously terrible at doing an English accent. It is doubtful that Cubby thought that Dick Van Dyke was really a viable candidate and this sounds more like Dick Van Dyke just telling an amusing anecdote than anything concrete or credible. In mitigation though, Cubby seemed to ask just about everyone he met if they'd like to test for Bond so you never know!

It is often reported that Simon Dee was invited to test for OHMSS. In the late 1960s, Dee was a young BBC chat show host and one of the most famous people in Britain. Dee was seen as one of the hippest symbols of Swinging Sixties London. Though he made appearances in The Italian Job and Doctor in Trouble, Dee did not become an actor or come into serious consideration for OHMSS. A few years later he moved to ITV but the failure of his chat show there effectively ended his career. A small irony here is that the show which more or less put the final nail in Simon Dee's career came when he interviewed George Lazenby and allowed (a rather addled and spaced out) Lazenby to confusingly waffle on about President Kennedy and conspiracy theories.

Another ludicrous alleged candidate was the singer Tom Jones (who of course sang the theme song to Thunderball). Jones claims that he was considered for the part but that common sense prevailed in the end and he was wisely ruled out of contention. "When I was young I would have liked to be James Bond, and at one time it was discussed," said Jones in 2010. "I think it came from Cubby Broccoli, who was the man in charge, of course, and he said when my name was put forward - 'Tom Jones is so recognisable as Tom Jones - he's a character, he's become this singer with a big character. So in order for him to do James Bond, would people accept him as being James Bond? Could they get past him being Tom Jones?' - and so apparently that was what the problem was." Yes, I think it's probably safe to say that Tom Jones playing Bond was a concept unlikely to fly very far!

The actor Eric Braeden, a regular face on American television and about to star in the western 100 Rifles (with Raquel Welch, Burt Reynolds and Jim Brown), said that he was courted to play Bond in OHMSS but that Cubby Broccoli and Harry Saltzman lost interest when they learned that he was German. Braeden was sort of Bondish in terms of his looks. He had black hair and was quite a handsome man - in a slightly exotic way. You may have seen him in films like Escape from the Planet of the Apes, Colossus: The Forbin Project, and Titanic. Braeden was still in his twenties when OHMSS was being planned.

Another foreign actor who was considered for OHMSS was the Canadian Daniel Pilon. Pilon was twenty-nine and had just appeared in the Michael Caine film Play Dirty for Harry Saltzman. Saltzman saw a lot of Bond potential in Pilon and courted him for the part. However, in an interview many years later, Pilon said that while Harry Saltzman was keen on him the same could not be said for Cubby Broccoli and so his chances of playing Bond in OHMSS were always pretty remote. Eric Braeden and Daniel Pilon both became familiar faces in US soap operas later in their career.

One obvious person to test for James Bond at this time was
Tom Adams. Adams starred in three James Bond copycat films
- Licensed to Kill (1965) and the sequels Where the Bullets Fly
(1966) and Somebody's Stolen Our Russian Spy (1967). In
these movies Adams played a secret agent named Charles
Vine. Adams had a very 1960s Milk Tray Man sort of look and
was good with action and fight scenes. It has been reported
that he tested for Bond more than once in the 1960s. Adams
also had a part in the Raquel Welch spy comedy Fathom and
later became a familiar face to British television viewers
thanks to his role in The Onedin Line. Like Patrick Allen and
William Franklyn, Adams made the most out of his theatrical
voice in later years. He fronted many commercials and became
the voice of E4.

The Greek actor George Fountas was - to his surprise - asked
to audition for the part of Bond in OHMSS. Fountas had only
really worked in Greece but someone at EON obviously
thought he had a good look for the part and might be worth a
punt. Fountas later said he was interested in the role but that
his 007 chances were nixed by not having sufficient time to
improve his English enough to be a realistic option. Fountas
was in his early forties at the time so his age might have been a
factor that went against him. A lot of the actors they tested for
OHMSS were much younger than Fountas.

Patrick Mower, if he is to be believed, tested for James Bond
several times and OHMSS was his first crack at the part.
Mower had just appeared in the horror film The Devil Rides
Out and was starting to secure roles in British television.
Mower had a roguish charm and a decent enough look for
Bond with his shock of black hair and dimpled chin. "I was the
first person to be told Sean wasn't returning to the role," said
Mower. "Sean was a super, super star. Back then he was God. I
couldn't believe it when the producers called me in and asked
if I'd like to do it. I was 28. They tested me as they thought I
was too young. And I did, too. I mean, Sean was a man and I
still saw myself as a little boy."

Another young actor who was interviewed about playing Bond in OHMSS was Anthony Valentine. He was in his late twenties. Valentine was in the TV show Callan at the time and would appear in gazillions of films and television productions (including a stint as Raffles in the 1970s). Though a very likeable screen presence it is doubtful that Valentine had quite the right looks or charisma to be James Bond. You can't quite picture him as James Bond - although he could be believably tough and cold. Anthony Valentine later narrated some James Bond audiobooks.

Another young actor EON looked at was Michael Billington. Billington was twenty-seven at the time and had only a few credits to his name. He would become fairly famous in the next few years thanks to his role in the Gerry Anderson sci-fi show UFO. "I suppose my involvement began in the mid sixties when Bud Ornstein, then Head of Production at United Artists in Europe, saw me in late night theatre and asked me to meet with him at the U.A. Offices," said Billington. "He told me that he would get some photographs done and show them to Harry Saltzman. Some weeks later I was called in for a Meeting by Dyson Lovell to meet with Peter Hunt for On Her Majesty's Secret Service; but I believed from my 'insider' that they already had George Lazenby under contract yet clearly hoped Connery would capitulate. When I saw a photograph of Lazenby I thought he had the perfect look for the role, so subsequently I put it out of my mind." Billington would be a much more serious James Bond candidate in the seventies and early eighties.

Also on the EON radar was a thirtysomething Ian Richardson - who was already a respected stage and film actor. Richardson was one of many actors who was considered for OHMSS but did not make the final auditions. Richardson's most famous role came years later as the shrewd but ruthless politician Francis Urquhart in the BBC's House of Cards. Richardson always seemed much more suited to playing Sherlock Holmes than James Bond so it was perhaps no surprise that he later played the Great Detective in two 1980s television movies.

OHMSS marked the first time that David Warbeck was vaguely in the running to become James Bond. Warbeck was twenty-eight at the time and had come over to Britain in 1965 from his native New Zealand to study acting. After a stint as a model Warbeck had begun to pick up some television work and was about to make his film debut playing the title role in Wolfshead: The Legend of Robin Hood (a low-budget offering from director John Hough which was supposed to be a television pilot but got a theatrical release). "All that froth going on!" said David Warbeck of On Her Majesty's Secret Service. "They were seeing everybody. I went along just to meet the director and sort of argued with them that I was quite wrong. But when I heard the blokes that were going for it I thought, well, why not me? No, I was still still too young."

After what seemed a lifetime, the producers finally managed to whittle down the Bond candidates to five finalists. These candidates were all given a full costumed screen test and essentially made to fight it out for the most famous role in cinema. LIFE Magazine sent photographer Loomis Dean to the casting sessions and in the October 1968 issue of the magazine all of the candidates were shown in a fascinating series of black and white photographs as they did their tests or just relaxed off camera. Peter Hunt directed the tests and the candidates were required to perform a fight with a heavy and also the scene where Tracy di Vicenzo pulls a gun on Bond in the hotel room.

The first candidate was Dutch born Hans De Vries. De Vries was twenty-seven and obviously must have already known Harry Saltzman quite well because he had small roles in two Saltzman produced films - You Only Live Twice and Billion Dollar Brain. His other credits included The Saint and Doctor Who. De Vries was dark-haired and quite sullen looking. He sort of looked the part of Bond but all the same you feel like the producers could still do better and find someone more patently Bondian. Hans De Vries obviously did not get the part of James Bond in the end and quietly faded into obscurity. He had his last acting credit in 1974. De Vries obviously decided that acting wasn't for him and went off to do something else.

The next candidate was Anthony Rogers. His date of birth seems elusive but he does look somewhat more mature than the other candidates in the test photographs. Rogers was probably the least Bondian of the candidates in terms of his looks. His hair was slightly wavy and curly (with a hint of encroaching silver) and he had a smirk that seemed to dominate his entire face when it broke out. He did look quite distinguished though. Rogers looked like the sort of person they'd cast as the lead in a 1950s science fiction adventure. Anthony Rogers was born in Scotland and moved to the United States as a young man where he became a water sports instructor and dabbled in theatre. He returned home and got a part in Doctor Who before going back to the United States to appear in the action show Combat.

In 1965, Rogers appeared in the Howard Hawks motor racing film Red Line 7000. A few years later he also appeared in the Howard Hawks western El Dorado and the musical costume drama Camelot (in which Richard Harris was the star). Anthony Rogers was obviously not cast as Bond in the end. Just like with Hans De Vries, Rogers seemed to vanish into thin air soon after his OHMSS auditions. It's like those OHMSS final auditions were cursed! Rogers evidently did not decide to stick with acting. For the purposes of this book, I watched Anthony Rogers in Combat and though he looks quite good it's debatable if that look was suited to 007. His acting was also not entirely convincing.

Another of the finalists was a young American named Robert Campbell. Campbell was probably the most traditionally handsome of all the candidates. With his black hair and heroic dimpled chin, Campbell definitely LOOKED like James Bond but his acting abilities were apparently not quite up to par because he wasn't chosen. Campbell was the most enigmatic of the candidates (and that's saying something!) in that absolutely nothing is known about his acting career or if he even had one. He was best known for being the brother of a television actor called William Campbell. Robert Campbell is a mystery wrapped up in an enigma. All we know is that as a young man he looked very James Bondish. While this got him a Bond audition though he didn't end up with the keys to the Aston Martin.

The next candidate was a twenty-nine year-old Australian named George Lazenby. Believe it or not, George Lazenby came on the radar of EON when Cubby Broccoli noticed him in his hairdressers! Lazenby, unless you count a Big Fry chocolate commercial, wasn't even an actor. He had rather blagged his way to an audition by pretending to be a playboy and actor. "I had no acting experience," said Lazenby. "I was coming from the male model point of view. I walked in looking like James Bond, and acting as if that's the way I was anyway. And they thought, 'All we have to do is keep this guy just the way he is and we'll have James Bond.'" When he auditioned to play James Bond, Lazenby accidentally broke the nose of stuntman/wrestler Yuri Borienko with a wild punch during the fight scene part his audition. George Lazenby seemed like someone who could handle himself in a real fight and this impressed the Bond people.

Lazenby had a fantastic look for Bond. He looked exactly like you'd imagine a sixties playboy or superhero spy to look like. He had swagger, moved well, could handle himself in a fight, and was exceptionally fit and athletic. Lazenby obviously had little acting experience but Peter Hunt did not think this would be an insurmountable obstacle. He felt that with the right direction and a competent and experienced leading lady then Lazenby's inexperience could be negated and he would simply come across as this fantastic looking new James Bond. Lazenby was very much in the Connery template in terms of his look. Peter Hunt and Cubby Broccoli were both fairly convinced that Lazenby was the best candidate and the obvious person to cast but there was still one more contender to go. This last contender turned out to be Lazenby's closest rival for the coveted part of 007.

John Richardson was in his mid-thirties and best known for starring in the films She and One Million Years B.C. Richardson had appeared in over a dozen films and was by far the most experienced and competent actor out of the five candidates. He was blue-eyed and handsome and very Milk Tray Man. Richardson's main flaw was his hair (he seems to have an elaborate comb over going on in the tests) but that wasn't really a problem because Connery wore a toupee as Bond and no doubt Richardson would of worn one as well. John Richardson seems preposterously thin in the auditions but this wasn't really a problem either as it would have been easy for him and gain weight and bulk up had he been cast.

Richardson seemed like a pretty good candidate to the producers and they were slightly torn on whether to go with him or Lazenby. In the end though they backed their instincts and felt that Lazenby had the edge. John Richardson did not vanish into complete obscurity like the other finalists but his acting career never really seemed to get much traction after the early promise. He later made a number of cheapjack films in Italy. EON did not forget John Richardson though. In fact, as we shall see later, there is evidence that he was considered for the part again in the early seventies.

George Lazenby was cast as James Bond only weeks before On Her Majesty's Secret Service began production. When Lazenby replaced Sean Connery as Bond, they were originally going to say that Bond had plastic surgery to fool his enemies as a means to explain why James Bond didn't look like Sean Connery anymore! However, this idea was sensibly abandoned in the end. Audiences were well aware that the actor had changed. When Lazenby turned up to Pinewood Studios for the first day of shooting a security guard failed to recognise him and wouldn't let him in. That was more or less Lazenby's Bond career in a nutshell. He was the 'other fella' sandwiched between the large shadows cast by Sean Connery and Roger Moore.

On Her Majesty's Secret Service, the first Bond film not to feature Sean Connery, is often written about as if it was a dreadful failure but this was not the case. Sure, audiences at the time unavoidably missed Sean Connery but the film made some money and is now felt by many fans (and I would include myself among them) to be the best James Bond movie ever made. It should be noted that Connery probably wouldn't have mustered much enthusiasm for OHMSS even if he had somehow been lured back. Besides, one of the strengths of the film was that Lazenby's youth and inexperience gave him a vulnerability which wouldn't have been so believable if conveyed by Connery's Bond. Oddly enough, Lazenby, though an inferior actor, actually suited the more human story of OHMSS more than Connery.

Strangely, it's not that difficult to watch OHMSS and just accept this is still Connery's Bond only with a different actor - and the film is determined to run with that concept, even linking the title sequence into the Connery films. Lazenby was chosen because of his physical similarities to Connery. As with Connery, Lazenby was also believably tough and had a rough and ready sort of quality. After George Lazenby declined an invitation to return as James Bond in Diamonds Are Forever, he was frozen as the 'one-off Bond' and it was often wrongly assumed that both Lazenby and OHMSS had been a failure. Over time though, the strengths of the film have been rightly acknowledged.

On Her Majesty's Secret Service was rare in the Bond franchise in that it was a relatively faithful adaptation of a Fleming novel. This meant that OHMSS had an amazingly downbeat and bold ending for a Bond film. The original plan for On Her Majesty's Secret Service was to end with Bond's wedding and then have Tracy killed in the PTS of the next movie. The director Peter Hunt dug his heels in though and insisted that OHMSS should have a downbeat ending. OHMSS is arguably the most human Bond film ever made and also has beautiful Alpine locations, the peerless Diana Rigg, fantastic action sequences, and a wondrous John Barry score. On Her

Majesty's Secret Service grossed $82 million from a $7 million budget. It was far from a flop.

One could plausibly argue that On Her Majesty's Secret Service is the best James Bond film EON have ever made. In 2013, the film director Steven Soderbergh went into bat for OHMSS and argued this very case when he said - "Shot to shot, this movie is beautiful in a way none of the other Bond films are — the anamorphic compositions are relentlessly arresting — and the editing patterns of the action sequences are totally bananas; it's like Peter Hunt took all the ideas of the French new wave and blended them with Eisenstein in a Cuisinart to create a grammar that still tops today's how fast can you cut aesthetic, because the difference here is that each of the shots — no matter how short — are real shots, not just additional coverage from the hosing-it-down school of action, so there is a unification of the aesthetic of the first unit and the second unit that doesn't exist in any other Bond film. And, speaking of action, there are as many big set pieces in OHMSS as any Bond film ever made, and if that weren't enough, there's a great score by John Barry, some really striking sound work, and what can you say about Diana Rigg that doesn't start with the word WOW?"

George Lazenby had wrongly assumed he would be awash with offers after playing Bond. The problem for Lazenby though is that he wasn't an actor. His performance in OHMSS, guided by the director Peter Hunt and the supporting class of Diana Rigg, was remarkably good given his inexperience. But he had no acting career to fall back on. Aside from a Big Fry chocolate commercial, Lazenby had no acting CV at all before Bond. Sean Connery, Roger Moore, Timothy Dalton, Pierce Brosnan, and Daniel Craig were all professional actors when they were hired as Bond. They all had, to varying degrees, a body of work (Connery was actually the most inexperienced out of the five because he was only 30 when he became Bond) behind them and a career to fall back on. Lazenby was never willing to serve his apprenticeship - something that the other Bond actors all had to do before they became rich and famous.

The most remarkable thing about Lazenby's departure from Bond is that he genuinely seemed to believe he was leaving a sinking ship. His agent Ronan O'Rahilly told him that James Bond was conservative and out of vogue. A dust shrouded relic of the fifties that would wheeze on for a couple more films and then be consigned to cinematic history. It was one of the stupidest pieces of advice anyone could ever be unfortunate enough to receive. Ronan O'Rahilly wrecked Lazenby's acting career and cost him millions with this knuckleheaded prediction.

The interesting thing about On Her Majesty's Secret Service is that it showed the Bond formula was more flexible than might have been suspected. Compared to gargantuan tongue-in-cheek extravaganzas like Thunderball and You Only Live Twice, OHMSS was surprisingly dramatic and emotional. It presented Bond not as an indestructible superhero but as someone who could have his heart broken. OHMSS was the first film in the franchise that explored the concept of making Bond more human. However, whether it was the box-office (which was decent enough but a considerable drop from You Only Live Twice) or the fallout from Lazenby affair, the producers were in no rush to repeat the experiment. It would be seventeen years before the Bond franchise attempted to make Bond more human again.

Peter Hunt felt that George Lazenby would have made a great Bond if he'd stuck with the franchise. "Had George Lazenby been more sensible, and had Broccoli and Saltzman been more sensible with him, I think he would have made a very credible Bond. He was a great looking guy and he moved along very well, although he wasn't really an actor. He was a model who had not done any acting before that. I think if things had gone the other way, he would have gone on to be a very good Bond."

Though the film turned out to be excellent, the production of OHMSS was not the happiest of times. Lazenby irritated the producers by acting as if he was a big star and sulking when he didn't get his way on something. Lazenby and Peter Hunt fell out to the point where they hardly spoke on the set. There were press stories of a feud between Lazenby and Diana Rigg which were overblown but did have some grains of truth. Lazenby later said he was annoyed that Rigg acted as if she was the star of the film. You can though rather forgive Diana Rigg if this was the case because she WAS more famous than Lazenby and a big star in her own right! Rigg was not only immortal as Emma Peel but a serious stage actress. The Bond producers were very lucky to have her in OHMSS and her performance was superb.

Lazenby, despite the ill informed perceptions of him as the failed one-off Bond, was surprisingly good in OHMSS. He really should have stuck with the part and made a least a couple more films. It was completely insane of Lazenby to turn his back on 007 and walk away. Lazenby was actually forwarded part of his salary for Diamonds Are Forever before he quit. He had to return the money. The news that George Lazenby had quit Bond franchise leaked before On Her Majesty's Secret Service was released. As a consequence, the promotional campaign downplayed Lazenby and billed James Bond as the star. This was very different from the Connery films - which also made a big deal of declaring that Sean Connery IS James Bond.

Lazenby, to the annoyance of Cubby Broccoli, turned up to the OHMSS premiere looking scruffy with long hair and a beard. It felt like a suitably strange coda to Lazenby's brief tenure as James Bond. Lazenby only discovered that George Baker had dubbed some of his OHMSS dialogue (where 007 poses as genealogist Sir Hilary Bray) when he watched the film at the premiere. Lazenby was not best pleased by this.

In one of his last interviews, the Q actor Desmond Llewelyn said of George Lazenby - "I know about George from what he has told me later. He wasn't an actor, he was a car salesman. It was jolly bad luck with him really. When he met Cubby and he asked him to do a test, he had never met an actor and didn't know what a test was. He spent a couple of days looking for actors, to find out what happened. Then some idiot said you're a star now behave like one. He had only read in the papers how stars behaved off the set, such as getting drunk and having a good time. What he didn't realise was on the set they were highly professional people, they didn't argue with the director, they learnt their lines, they were on time. Lazenby just behaved extremely badly."

Adjusted for inflation in today's money, Lazenby was paid about $400,000 for On Her Majesty's Secret Service. He was by far the lowest paid Bond actor. This made his decision to walk away from Bond after one film even more crazy. He should have done a couple more Bond films and then at least he could have walked away with a few million in the bank! George Lazenby naively presumed OHMSS had made him a star and that he would now go off on his merry way as a successful and much in demand actor. However, much to his dismay you'd imagine, Lazenby was suddenly plunged into absolute obscurity.

"After the Bond fiasco nobody would touch me", said Lazenby. "Harry Saltzman had always said, If you don't do another Bond you'll wind up doing spaghetti westerns in Italy. But I couldn't even get one of those. My agent couldn't believe it. But the word was out – I was difficult." In an interview in 1969, Diana Rigg was asked about Lazenby walking away from James Bond and said that he must be crazy. "The role made Sean Connery a millionaire. It made Sean Connery. I truly don't know what's happening in George's mind so I can only speak of my reaction. I think it's a pretty foolish move. I think if he can bear to do an apprenticeship, which everybody in this business has to do – has to do – then he should do it quietly and with humility. Everybody has to do it. There are few instant successes in the film business. And the instant successes one usually associates with somebody who is willing to learn anyway."

After he quit the Bond franchise, Lazenby took some acting

lessons in an attempt to boost his career. It didn't really make much difference. A 1971 drama about gun runners called Universal Soldier (in which Lazenby played a hippie mercenary in London) was partly funded by Lazenby but completely bombed. Lazenby spent the rest of the seventies making cheapie Hong Kong action flicks and Australian television movies. Lazenby claimed that after he quit the Bond franchise, Cubby Broccoli used his influence to have Lazenby shunned in the film industry. It's obviously impossible to verify these allegations.

George Lazenby had failed to deduce the simple and universal fact that no actor was bigger than James Bond. Lazenby assumed he was a star after OHMSS but James Bond was the star. By leaving the Bond series after one film, Lazenby stupidly pressed the self-destruct button his own acting career before it had even begun. Many decades later, Lazenby could probably allow himself to see the funny side as he signed autographs at Bond conventions and did yet another interview about his time as James Bond. Fads and eras (not to mention actors) come and go but James Bond was indestructible and forever. Lazenby now knew that only too well.

DIAMONDS ARE FOREVER

Before George Lazenby quit the Bond franchise after one movie, Richard Maibaum wrote a treatment for Diamonds are Forever in which Bond seeks revenge on Blofeld for the murder of his wife in On Her Majesty's Secret Service. Irma Bunt and Marc Ange Draco returned in the treatment. Cubby Broccoli was said to have disliked the story though and when Lazenby vacated the role of 007 the notion of doing a direct sequel to On Her Majesty's Secret Service lost a lot of its currency anyway.

The Bond producers and United Artists now faced their ultimate nightmare. They had to find a new James Bond actor much sooner than expected. It must have felt like the dust had only just settled on the endless interviews, readings, and auditions for OHMSS but now they had to do it all over again! One name who again couldn't be considered was Roger Moore. Moore began shooting the television show The Persuaders with Tony Curtis in 1970 and was unavailable. Another actor who wasn't considered for Diamonds Are Forever was Timothy Dalton. Dalton still felt far too young to even think about playing Bond. Besides, at this time Dalton had turned his back on films and gone back to the theatre for a time. He'd dropped off the radar somewhat.

It appears that none of the finalists for the part of Bond in OHMSS were considered for Diamonds Are Forever. Some new candidates were therefore required. But where to start? What sort of Bond should they be looking for? Another Connery/Lazenby type or someone different for the new decade? This was not an easy question to answer. Peter Anthony, the model who won the Daily Express competition to discover a James Bond for Dr No, was apparently brought back to do a test for Diamonds Are Forever. Anthony was more mature now and still looked the part but his acting wasn't much better than it had been in 1961 so he was rejected for the second time.

Some other previous candidates were also considered for Diamonds Are Forever. Harry Saltzman was still quite interested in Michael Billington. Around this time Saltzman hired Gerry Anderson to write a script treatment for an adaption of Ian Fleming's Moonraker and there was some speculation about Billington playing Bond in this film (which obviously didn't go ahead in the end).

* Billington does not seem to have become a serious candidate for Diamonds Are Forever. It could be that his youth and television commitments precluded him from becoming a stronger candidate. Next time around though Billington would come within a whisker of the part.

David Warbeck was again briefly considered. Warbeck was having a pretty good run at the time. He was set for appearances in Twins of Evil and A Fistful of Dynamite and had appeared in two episodes of UFO. Warbeck wasn't the most outlandishly handsome Bond candidate but he was rather dashing and had something about him. Another person who EON hadn't forgotten was Patrick Mower. Michael Gambon claimed that Cubby Broccoli wanted to cast Mower as Bond in Diamonds Are Forever but this was blocked by United Artists because they didn't want another inexperienced unknown like Lazenby. While you can understand that the studio were eager to hire someone with stature and fame it seems a little harsh on Mower as by 1970 he was a very experienced actor - certainly in comparison to Lazenby.

As for Michael Gambon, he was (to his great surprise), asked if he wanted to test to play Bond in Diamonds Are Forever by Cubby Broccoli. Gambon was thirty yers-old at the time and more of a stage than screen actor (in fact, he had only made one film). "I was given a smoked-salmon sandwich and a glass of champagne," said Gambon, "and Cubby said: 'We're looking for a new James Bond.' And I started laughing. 'James Bond, me? I'm not the right shape.' He said: 'Well, we have ice bags for Sean's chest and your jowls, doesn't take more than two days and the recovery period's a week. Teeth, well we can do that in an afternoon. And Sean wears a piece. I'll get a toupee for you'!" Despite this, Gambon was sensible enough not to pursue the matter. He is a great actor but it's hard to see him as Bond. Michael Gambon was more evidence that Cubby Broccoli had a weakness for asking virtually everyone he met to test for James Bond!

The late Adam West said that he met Cubby Broccoli around this time and was asked if he'd be interested in playing James Bond in the next film. Cubby's wife Dana Broccoli confirmed that Adam West was indeed approached regarding Bond around the time that Diamonds Are Forever was being planned. West was forty-two years-old and had just finished his memorable stint as Batman in the enjoyably tongue-in-cheek television show. The idea of Adam West as James Bond sounds laughable on the face of it (and it was always rather unlikely) but maybe it wasn't as ridiculous as it sounds. It's not as if Adam West wasn't a handsome chap good at portraying playboys. West was very suave (you might even venture he was sort of like the American version of Roger Moore!) and knew his way around a quip. It doesn't take an impossible leap of imagination to picture Adam West in a campy tongue-in-cheek sort of Bond film and that's exactly the sort of film that Diamonds Are Forever turned out to be! Nonetheless, Adam West declined the invitation to be considered for Bond. He felt that James Bond should be played by a British actor. West, as we shall see, would not be the last American Bond candidate to make this observation.

A British actor seriously considered for Diamonds Are Forever was Michael McStay. McStay was 37 and looked a bit like Clark Kent in a Superman comic. McStay had been in a couple of films but most of his CV consisted of television work. Among the shows he'd appeared in were The Avengers, Z-Cars, and Dixon of Dock Green. There was a lot of media speculation in 1970 that McStay might be the next Bond. "There was an article in the paper saying one of these six actors is James Bond and I was one of them," said McStay. "I'd been through a fair selection process, the only thing I hadn't done was a film test. Then I got a phone call call from a reporter in the Far East who said he'd got a cable saying Michael McStay is the next Bond. My agent heard nothing about it, couldn't confirm it, the press arrived at my house in force." Michael McStay was obviously not chosen in the end although it appears that the producers were interested in him. McStay continued to be a prolific television actor in the decades to come. He has been in everything from Doctor Who to Coronation Street to The Bill.

An unlikely but interesting candidate for Diamonds Are Forever was Roger Green. Green was a former rugby player from New Zealand who became a meat importer. He ended up drifting into acting after meeting the writer Robert Bolt at a party. Green credited a theatrical agent named Johnny

Harrison for getting him a meeting with Cubby Broccoli and Harry Saltzman. Green was something of a real life James Bond as his job took him to dangerous places and he was fond of booze and the playboy lifestyle. He was tall and dark-haired and had a decent enough look for Bond. Green did a screen test for the director Guy Hamilton (who was returning to the franchise for the first time since Goldfinger) in which he played a scene with the doomed Carry On actress Imogen Hassall. In the test Hassall played Tiffany Case while Bob Simmons played Peter Franks. It was the classic Bond audition scenario. Green had to show he could be suave with the ladies and then have a punch up!

Roger Green said that Guy Hamilton was very complimentary about his screen test and predicted he was in with a good shout of getting the part. Whether or not Hamilton was just being polite is hard to say. Roger Green's screen test is one of the few that is now public and can be viewed online. While he can obviously handle himself in a scrap and sort of looks the part you wouldn't say that Green displayed much in the way of acting ability, charm, or charisma. Roger Green said that as someone who wasn't really an actor he was realistic enough to realise that his chances were slim but nonetheless he got his hopes up because he was still in contention even when many other candidates had been rejected. In the end green's hopes were dashed by the return of Sean Connery. Green believes that United Artists would never had sanctioned hiring him anyway. "My agent said that Hamilton, Broccoli and Saltzman had wished me to play the role but United Artists had said, 'Not another unknown Antipodean actor please!'" In later years Green took advantage of his Bond connections to write a memoir which he titled Shaken & Stirred.

The suave American actor Robert Wagner said that Cubby Broccoli spoke to him about playing Bond in Diamonds Are Forever. Wagner was in his late thirties at the time and was still a reasonably big star (although he would do a lot more television work in the seventies). Wagner said that no official offer was made but Broccoli invited him to be considered for the part and said he could be a very good candidate. Wagner though, like Adam West, felt that he was too American to play James Bond and wouldn't be a good fit for the part at all. Wagner told Cubby Broccoli that he should go and hire Roger Moore (which was obviously something Cubby was unable to do at this time).

In a quirk of fate, many years later Roger Wagner married Jill St John - who played the female lead in Diamonds Are Forever. Jill St John and Lana Wood both play Bond girls in Diamonds Are Forever and there was a strange connection between these women some years later. Wagner used to be married to Lana's sister Natalie Wood. Natalie Wood drowned in 1981 while on a yacht with Robert Wagner and Lana has always suspected foul play in her sister's death. There is another bizarre Bond connection to this story because the third person on the yacht that tragic night was Christopher Walken.

Among the more unlikely candidates to play Bond in Diamonds Are Forever was Malcom Roberts. Roberts was a twenty-six year-old singer who had three hit singles in the late 1960s.

Roberts was looked at by the producers but does not appear to have been seriously considered. Roberts had actually began his career as an actor and once appeared in Coronation Street. Roberts had blonde hair and a very large comic book chin. He looked a bit like a much larger and heavier version of Adam Faith. Roberts later attempted to represent the United Kingdom in the 1991 Eurovision Song Contest but didn't get picked. It has been alleged that Robert Powell was a candidate to play Bond in Diamonds Are Forever although Powell said that he never received a formal approach. Powell was in his late twenties at the time and had appeared in a number of TV shows and a few films (most notably The Italian Job). Robert Powell was a very competent actor but you probably can't really imagine him as James Bond.

Perhaps the strongest new candidate EON managed to find was 38 year-old Simon Oates. Oates had appeared in all manner of TV shows (everything from Armchair Theatre to The Avengers) and a few films too. Oates was the lead actor in the daft 1967 Amicus sci-fi film the Terrornauts and while The Terrornauts is a pretty terrible film (though you might describe it as a guilty pleasure) Oates is actually very good in it and a likeable and relaxed screen presence. He looked good too and was tall and urbane. In fact, in 1971, Oates even played John Steed in an Avengers stage show. He was a very suave chap. Oates had just begun a stint in the ecological sci-fi series Doomwatch in 1970 but was still permitted to test for Diamonds Are Forever. By all accounts, Oates came pretty close to bagging the part of 007.

"I nearly got the James Bond role in 1971 and missed out on it, unluckily, because Sean came back and decided to do one more!" said Oates in one of his last interviews. "I did the audition and got a round of applause from everybody in the studio. They were all very pleased and things looked very positive. Cubby Broccoli was talking terms with my agent - and then one day, he telephoned me. 'Sorry, Simon. Sean's coming back,' he said. I understood. Connery was Bond and if he wanted to do it again, they really couldn't turn him down in favour of Simon Oates, could they? When the next one (Live and Let Die) came up, I was working, so I lost Bond - I couldn't do it. Mind you, the way my life's gone, playing Bond would have changed the course of it and I wouldn't be where I am now. In the end, I'm grateful that I didn't do it. I've had a smashing career and I'm very happy."

Simon Oates was not though the actor who came closest to the part of James Bond in Diamonds Are Forever. That accolade went to the American actor John Gavin. Gavin has the unusual distinction of being the only actor who signed to play James Bond but never actually made a Bond film! For a brief moment in time, John Gavin was officially signed on the dotted line to play James Bond in Diamonds Are Forever. Gavin was forty years-old and certainly looked the part. He was handsome, dark-haired, and muscular. Gavin made his film debut in 1956 and was probably best known for playing Sam Loomis in Hitchcock's Psycho. Gavin had also played Julius Caesar in Kubrick's Spartacus and appeared in Thoroughly Modern Millie with Julie Andrews.

What probably landed Gavin the Bond role was the 1968 film OSS 117 – Double Agent. OSS 117 – Double Agent was what you might describe as a Spaghetti spy film and one of the many European James Bond mimics or parodies that festooned the 1960s. OSS 117 is Hubert Bonisseur de La Bath, a fictional secret agent created by French writer Jean Bruce. A number of actors have played this character in tongue-in-cheek and Bondish parodies. The producers clearly watched Gavin in this spy spoof and thought he would make a passable Bond. The signing of Gavin was a surprise mainly because he was American. Gavin was also no Laurence Olivier and his signing seemed somewhat of an act of desperation - as if EON were struggling to find an actor so just picked the most James Bondish looking person they could find and didn't worry about whether he could act or not. "Time was getting awfully short", said Cubby Broccoli. "We had to have someone in the bullpen."

United Artists were not enthused at all by the selection of John Gavin. They saw Gavin as an actor who was on the slide as his recent projects had included a failed television western film pitched as a pilot for a proposed show and a supporting role in the megabomb comedy Pussycat, Pussycat, I Love You. The studio, still bruised by the Lazenby affair, wanted someone more famous than John Gavin to play Bond. United Artists decided that the only thing to do was to get Sean Connery back - at any cost. This required the studio to pay a then unheard of fee amounting to $1.25 million (which Connery donated to charity), finance two film projects of Connery's choice **, and also pay the actor compensation for any overrun in the weekly shooting schedule.

It was a sensational deal at the time and illustrated that as far as United Artists were concerned the Bond franchise was simply not viable without Sean Connery. The unlucky John Gavin was compensated financially by the studio for the termination of his contract and drifted into television roles. In 1981 he became the United States Ambassador to Mexico. "It was a business agreement—with our consent of course," said Cubby Broccoli of removing Gavin as Bond to make way for Connery. "So we accepted that fact that Sean is Bond—but not that John is not. I think John Gavin will be eligible for the James Bond role when it comes up again."

Diamonds Are Forever saw a big lurch in tone towards tongue-in-cheek humour after the more sombre and tragic events of On Her Majesty's Secret Service. While purists might have been dismayed by this shift to a more campy and flippant type of Bond film, from a commercial point of view it made sense and the flaws in the movie were mitigated by the delight audiences felt at Sean Connery's return. The plot of Diamonds Are Forever is vague to the extreme and some of the special effects are strangely mediocre for a James Bond production (the satellite set-piece is atrocious) but the feeling of aimlessness that seems to dog Diamonds Are Forever is compensated for by some fun escapism - like the oil pipe sequence, Bond's fight in the elevator, the Las Vegas car stunt (where the Mustang famously comes out of the alleyway the wrong way up), and the large scale oil rig battle sequence at the end.

A 40 year-old Sean Connery is clearly coasting in Diamonds are Forever. He's a little bit pudgy and has the air of a man who is impatient to get back to the golf course. However, he is of course terrific muttering the deadpan quips supplied by Tom Mankiewicz. The film has an enjoyably surreal atmosphere at times with the desert sequences and the famous Moon Buggysetpiece (Bond encountering a 'moon landing' in a television studio seems to be an early reference to those conspiracy theories that the moon landing was hoaxed). The score by John Barry is appropriately strange and makes a nice sonic backdrop for the action.

One of the disappointing things about Diamonds Are Forever though is that it barely mentions the events of OHMSS (where Blofeld and his goons murdered Bond's wife). Despite the return of Connery, part of you wishes Diamonds Are Forever was a direct follow-up to OHMSS with Lazenby. Diamonds Are Forever, with its humour and camp (Blofeld resorts to drag at one point), set the tone for the seventies Bond films to come. You could argue that Diamonds Are Forever feels a lot like the first Roger Moore Bond film - only without Roger Moore.

In 1971, as Diamonds Are Forever geared up for release, Sean Connery said of Cubby Broccoli and Harry Saltzman - "They're not exactly enamoured of each other. Probably because they're both sitting on fifty million dollars or pounds and looking across the desk at each other and thinking: that bugger's got half of what should be all mine." Connery is alleged to have had a clause inserted in his contract for Diamonds that Harry Saltzman wasn't allowed to go anywhere near him during the production. It's safe to say that Connery was no fan of the Bond producers and wouldn't miss them. Diamonds Are Forever was a tremendous financial success and did big business everywhere. But what was going to happen next? The chances of getting Connery back again seemed remote to say the least.

* Gerry Anderson later threatened legal action when The Spy Who Loved Me came out because he claimed it bore similarities to the Moonraker treatment he had written for Harry Saltzman several years previously. He was persuaded to drop his case in the end. The Moonraker script treatment that Gerry Anderson and Tony Barwick wrote for Harry Saltzman in the early 1970s had a villain named Zodiac and identical triplet henchmen. Zodiac was hijacking nuclear submarines in the story so you can see why Anderson threatened legal action when 1977's The Spy Who loved Me came out. "What happened was that Harry Saltzman phoned me and said 'Can you pop in? I'd like to see you'," said Anderson of his proposed version of Moonraker. "I went in and he said 'Gerry, I want you to produce the next Bond picture, Moonraker – here's the

book'. I nearly took off and went into orbit! I just thought it was a marvellous, marvellous break. I read the book, which frankly wasn't very exciting, and terribly out-of-date, as one would expect. I was initially trying to cement the deal, and at that time I would have put my thoughts together. What happened was that Tony Barwick – the late Tony Barwick, one of my favourite writers – and myself had written a synopsis. Harry had seen the synopsis and that was the reason he called me – he was fired by it. But a few weeks went by and then just the worst bit of luck in my life, I think! It was announced that Harry Saltzman was parting company with Cubby Broccoli. And so the thing went down the tubes."

** The disturbing 1973 crime drama The Offence (in which Connery well and truly sheds his James Bond image) was the only picture that resulted from this deal though. Connery had planned the other film to be an adaptation of Macbeth but this never got made in the end.

LIVE AND LET DIE

Before production began on the next Bond film - Live and Let Die - Tom Mankiewicz had lunch with Sean Connery in a charm offensive that EON hoped might persuade Connery to do the film. It was of course unsuccessful. "I always hear that it's my ******* obligation to play James Bond," Connery told Mankiewicz. "I've done six, when does my ******* obligation stop? After ten, twelve, fifteen?" Despite the best efforts of United Artists, Sean Connery decided that Diamonds Are Forever was definitely the end of his association with James Bond - until 1983 at least. He had grown weary of the role in the 1960s and found the fame and attention increasingly constrictive. As Connery pointed out, The Beatles had their fame spread over four people whereas with the James Bond craze it was him all on his own.

Connery simply wanted to do other things as an actor now. He didn't want to keep endlessly playing the same character all the time. It is said that United Artists (obviously to no avail) offered Connery $5 million to star in Live and Let Die. After they finished Diamonds Are Forever, the producers had the idea of bringing back Ursula Andress as Honey Ryder in the next movie. However, when Sean Connery made it clear he would not be coming back this idea was shelved. There wasn't much point in bringing back Ursula Andress if Connery wasn't doing the movie because it wouldn't be a reunion anymore.

For the third picture in a row, United Artists and Broccoli & Saltzman were faced with the unenviable task of finding a new actor to play James Bond. The studio wanted to cast Robert Redford as Bond after Sean Connery left for the second time but the chances of Redford accepting the role were close to zero. Redford was one of the biggest stars in Hollywood at the time so why would he want to constrict himself to Bond films when he had his pick of projects anyway? An American star who was definitely approached to take over as Bond was Clint Eastwood. Eastwood was not interested though. "I was offered pretty good money to do James Bond if I would take on the role," said Eastwood. "This was after Sean Connery left. My lawyer represented the Broccolis, and he came and said, 'They would love to have you.' But to me, well, that was somebody else's gig. That's Sean's deal. It didn't feel right for me to be doing it. I thought James Bond should be British. I am of British descent but by that same token, I thought that it should be more of the culture there and also, it was not my thing."

The director Guy Hamilton assumed that he was done with the Bond franchise after Diamonds Are Forever but he was persuaded to come back for Live and Let Die and once again found himself in charge of a film that had no leading man. Hamilton decided to have a bash at finding a Bond actor himself and remembered someone who he thought would be perfect. During the production of Diamonds Are Forever in the United States, Hamilton and the Bond producers had been introduced to the actor Burt Reynolds. Reynolds was in his mid-thirties and about to make the John Boorman film

Deliverance at the time. Guy Hamilton thought that Reynolds was terrific. The actor was good looking, tough, and could be charming and funny. In 1972, Hamilton proposed that they simply cast Burt Reynolds as Bond in Live and Let Die.

In years to come Burt Reynolds would become (for a time) the biggest box-office star in the world. He was most famous for car chase comedies and his moustache. It seems ludicrous to think of the comical Smokey & the Bandit version of Burt Reynolds as Bond but we are talking about the early seventies of Burt Reynolds before he became a big star.

If you watch something like Deliverance it's not that difficult to imagine Reynolds (with a Connery style toupee) playing James Bond. Sure, he was a bit on the short side (which could also be said of Daniel Craig!) and would have needed to work on the accent but Reynolds as Bond in 1972 wasn't a crazy suggestion at all. I can picture Reynolds as Bond in Live and Let Die and The Man with the Golden Gun although it is less easy to picture him in The Spy Who Loved Me or Moonraker.

The interest in Burt Reynolds was such that his agent was permitted to read the script for Live and Let Die. In the end though it was a combination of Cubby Broccoli and cold feet from Reynolds that stopped him from becoming the third official James Bond actor. Tom Mankiewicz said that Saltzman and Hamilton were happy to cast Reynolds but Cubby had second thoughts and insisted that Bond should be played by a British actor - which was something of a contradiction because Cubby had only recently cast an Australian and American as Bond! As for Burt Reynolds, he was reticent about taking the role and eventually backed out. "I think I could have done it well," said Reynolds. "In my stupidity, I said, 'An American can't play James Bond, it has to be an Englishman – Bond, James Bond. Nah, I can't do it.' Oops. Yeah, I could have done it. I would've liked to have had a shot at James Bond, if for no other reason, I'd be very rich now, and I could've had a good time."

As before, a number of previous candidates were wheeled back out and looked at again. John Richardson, who was nearly cast as Bond in OHMSS, was brought back and considered afresh. Richardson was about thirty-eight years old and was about to begin his era of making low-budget Italian films. He had though been in the 1970 Barbara Streisand film

On a Clear Day You Can See Forever. Richardson was still a very handsome man and with the right toupee would have been a terrific looking Bond. However, it was not to be for Richardson and he did not get the part again. The producers clearly liked Richardson though and on both occasions found him to be a viable and serious candidate for the role.

This was the last time that John Richardson was considered for Bond. The next time the Bond producers started seriously looking at alternative 007 candidates in the late seventies John Richardson was too old to be in contention.

The other familiar names back in the fray for Live and Let Die naturally included the inimitable David Warbeck. "I was more sure of myself," said Warbeck of his Live and Let Die test. "We had a script, walked in and met on the set. I said: How do you want this? Do you have anything in mind like the way it's gone before? No, he said, play it your way. We want to see how you're going to do it. So there I was, trying to be nice and cool, a few quips with the bird, then a whole fight scene after just a walk through of the choreography! That wrapped it up, we shook hands - bye!" Warbeck's test was to no avail and once again he failed to find the winning numbers for the 007 casting sweepstakes.

Also back was Patrick Mower. Mower said that he tested again for Bond in the early seventies but lost out to Roger Moore. This would obviously indicate that Mower was a candidate for Live and Let Die. Mower had recently appeared in the film Incense for the Damned (with Peter Cushing) and also Jason King and Black Beauty on television. Patrick Mower was one of those actors who never stopped working but had yet to find the role which propelled him to the next level. James Bond would obviously have done that but the 007 role would remain frustratingly elusive for Mower. The young Patrick Mower probably would have made a decent fist of Bond. There were certainly worse candidates down the decades.

John Ronane was another actor who was considered for Live and Let Die. Ronane was about thirty-eight at the time and had appeared in films such as King Rat and Charlie Bubbles.

His many television credits included (of course) The Avengers and The Saint. It seems slightly odd that if the producers liked Ronane they hadn't considered him for Diamonds Are Forever or OHMSS. Maybe they did. Ronane was not what you would describe as traditionally handsome or screamingly James Bondian in terms of looks but there was obviously something about him that EON liked. Ronane apparently did well in the Live and Let Die casting sweepstakes and was a serious candidate. He later moved to the United States and taught acting before returning home and appearing in TV shows like Juliet Bravo and Howard's Way.

Anthony Hopkins has said that he was approached by Cubby Broccoli with a view to playing James Bond in Live and Let Die. Hopkins was about 34 at the time and had just made the spy film When Eight Bells Toll. In the film Hopkins played British Treasury secret agent Phillip Calvert. The idea was that this would be the first in a new franchise of Phillip Calvert films but this never transpired in the end. The ironic thing is that Eight Bells Toll was designed to be a new gritty spy franchise to fill the gap left by Bond - which rival studios wrongly considered to be on its last legs and doomed without Sean Connery! Hopkins said that while it was very flattering to be approached about James Bond he did not pursue the part because he didn't feel he was right for it.

Very near the top of the EON wish list for Live and Let Die was Jon Finch. Finch was a brooding 30 year-old actor who resembled the wayward love child of Oliver Reed and Timothy

Dalton (Finch and Dalton sometimes even found themselves up for the same parts because of their similarities). Horror films The Vampire Lovers and The Horror of Frankenstein put Finch on the map and then he appeared in Roman Polanski's Macbeth and Alfred Hitchcock's brilliant suspense thriller Frenzy. Finch was quite an intense actor (note how Finch refuses to make his innocent wronged character in Frenzy sympathetic at all!) with a rich theatrical anachronistic voice. Not only that but he was a former paratrooper so the 007 style fights and stunts were not likely to be a problem at all. Finch even raced cars in his spare time. He was a pretty good candidate but - alas - he simply wasn't interested. A few years later Finch turned down a lead role in Richard Lester's The Three Musketeers. Jon Finch was clearly not that bothered about money and fame - which probably explains why he never became a big star.

William Gaunt was tested for the part of Bond in Live and let Die. Gaunt was 34 and already a television veteran (his credits naturally included Doctor Who and The Saint). From 1968 to 1969 he was one of the leads of the spy sci-fi show The Champions. Although he is a very good actor (who has done much stage work over the years) it's hard to picture Gaunt as James Bond. Gaunt looks too youthful in his photographs from this era. He looks like a little schoolboy and has none of the sex appeal and machismo one would associate with Bond. One can't imagine he was ever close to becoming a serious contender for Live and Let Die. British television viewers of a certain vintage might remember Gaunt best for the eighties BBC sitcom No Place Like Home. He continues to work on stage and the small screen and has been in everything from Eastenders to Midsomer Murders.

Guy Peters was a budding actor who had worked in commercials and the theatre. He found himself in the exciting position of meeting Cubby Broccoli and Guy Hamilton to discuss the part of James Bond in 1972. "My stage name at the time was Peter Laughton," said Peters in an interview for the website Alternative 007. "The reason for the stage name was that I am related to the late, great, actor Charles Laughton on my mother's side of the family. It came about that, on the 26th April, 1972, Mayfair (8, Hill Street) casting agent Alan Foenander, met me and thought I'd make a good Bond. He arranged a four way meeting between the producer Cubby Broccoli, director Guy Hamilton, himself and me. The meeting took place at EON productions' then headquarters at 2, South Audley Street, Mayfair on 1st May, 1972. My first impression of Cubby Broccoli and Guy Hamilton, when I walked into their office, was that they looked more like City types, in their dark suits, than my idea of a film men. I guess my idea of producers and directors was formed by seeing American film directors casually dressed in flowered shirts and wearing baseball caps!

"I felt that Guy Hamilton had a warmth about him and was very human. I liked him and could have worked with him. Cubby Broccoli, on the other hand, was a bit remote and unfathomable. At the interview, Cubby Broccoli asked me about military service. I pointed out that conscription was stopped one year before I would have been called up, so I never did National Service. However, I was a cadet in the ATC as a lad! He asked me about my acting experience in general and what parts I had played. I can't readily recall the whole conversation - after all, it was thirty nine years ago this month! Guy Hamilton asked me questions too. Cubby Broccoli said that had he met me when they were looking for a new face, they might have used me instead of Lazenby but, now, they might want a known face to play Bond. Afterwards, the man who had arranged the interview, Alan Foenander (casting agent), said that the interview went well and they would be in touch."

Guy Peters never heard back from EON. He never got as far as an audition. Interestingly, Peters said that at his interview Cubby Broccoli had told him that Roger Moore wouldn't be a candidate for James Bond because he was too associated with The Saint. That obviously didn't turn out to be true. Maybe it was misdirection on Cubby's part and he wanted to keep Roger's possible casting a secret? Guy Peters, on the evidence of his photos, was a fairly handsome and sturdy looking man and he had the requisite black hair. Whether or not he had the ability to play Bond though is something we will never know. He later went back into education and took a writing course.

An unlikely candidate to play Bond in Live and Let Die was Ranulph Fiennes. Fiennes was in his late twenties and an explorer who used to be in the SAS. You might argue that Fiennes became the greatest explorer in the world. Ranulph Fiennes was quite dashing as a young man although it is debatable if he had the right look for Bond. Of his experience testing for Live and Let Die, Fiennes said - "They decided that, rather than get an actor, they'd get someone who'd actually done all the Bond kind of stuff. Someone suggested me and I needed money for an expedition I was planning at the time, so I came down to London to see Cubby Broccoli. To my amazement, out of 400 people, I got down to the last six. Unfortunately, it only took two minutes for him to say, rather rudely, that I looked like "a farmer whose hands are too big and clumsy". So they chose Roger Moore instead."

It seems that John Gavin was looked at again for Live and Let Die although he doesn't appear to have been a serious candidate this time. It could be that Cubby Broccoli brought Gavin back into the 007 casting loop as a courtesy more than anything. If United Artists didn't like Gavin's casting in 1970 they were unlikely to have changed their minds two years later. It is sometimes alleged that George Lazenby was a contender for Live and Let Die - which would have been pretty strange! Although Lazenby was only in his early thirties his career was on life support and he said he suffered from alcoholism and two nervous breakdowns around this time. It seems very unlikely that United Artists and Cubby Broccoli would have welcomed Lazenby's return as Bond. As far as they were concerned Lazenby had burned his bridges.

Gary Myers was someone who caught the eye of EON around this time. Myers was a thirty one year-old model and actor who had appeared in the sci-fi show UFO (it seems that many

Bond candidates appeared in UFO!) but was best known for being the original Milk Tray Man in the Bondish Cadbury's chocolate adverts. What prevented Myers from becoming a serious candidate was his lack of acting experience. The fact that Myers was Australian probably didn't help at the time either. Although many actors from Australia were strong candidates to play Bond in years to come, in 1972 the Lazenby affair was still a sore point for EON so they probably weren't rushing to appoint another Australian quite so soon. Myer's acting credits seem to come to an abrupt end in 1973 so he obviously didn't stick with acting as a career.

Julian Glover was one of the actors who auditioned to play Bond in Live and Let Die. Glover was 37 at the time. A crisp and distinguished actor, Glover had enjoyed many television roles (he did the 'treble' in that he appeared in The Avengers, The Saint, and Doctor Who!) and would be a prolific film and television actor for decades to come.

Glover was probably most famous at the time for playing the pompous Colonel Breen in the excellent 1967 Hammer film Quatermass and the Pit. Glover said that he was one of several actors to test for Live and Let Die but felt that his audition wasn't very good.

"I was one of several people who were tested for James Bond," said Glover in 2020. "I think there were six of us. I didn't do a very good test I'm afraid and I didn't get the part. That was the end of that. At that time all six of us knew that it had to be Roger. When he was sitting there and waiting he was a living, breathing James Bond. Indeed we were right. I'm really glad that he got the part because he was brilliant Bond." Glover later played Kristatos in For Your Eyes Only. He was probably better at playing villains than heroes.

Jeremy Brett was another actor in contention for Live and Let Die. Brett may well have been considered for OHMSS too. Brett was nearly forty years-old in 1972 and an accomplished stage actor. He was probably best known at this time for appearing in the film My Fair Lady. Harry Saltzman was said to have been a big fan of Brett after watching My Fair lady and was an advocate of him doing Bond. Brett was tall, dark-haired and handsome and looked rather like the John McLusky sketch of Bond commissioned by Ian Fleming. It appears though that Cubby Broccoli wasn't so sold on Brett. It is possible that Broccoli thought that Brett might be a little too mannered and fey for Bond. There is no doubt though that Brett would have been capable of the elegance and cruelty of Bond. "It's the sort of role you cannot afford to turn down, but I think if I had got it, it would have spoiled me," said Brett of James Bond. Years later Brett would of course make a terrific Sherlock Holmes in the wonderful Granada series.

In the end only two actors were left standing after all the interviews, auditions, and screen tests for Live and Let Die. One of these was Michael Billington. Billington was 31 at the time and appearing in the TV show The Onedin Line. Live and Let Die was the first time that Billington actually did a screen test for James Bond. "I heard that Cubby Broccoli wanted to meet me with the prospect of a screen test," said Billington. "I was somewhat surprised. I was having some success on British Television at the time but really wanted to do a quality movie. I think I did well on the test for Live And Let Die and liked Guy Hamilton, the director. The scene was a specially written scene, which I played with an actress called Caroline Seymour. I heard from my agent's 'Insider' that there was going to be an offer made and there was some national press to that effect. When it was announced that Roger Moore was going to do it, I was stunned." Billington had a feeling though that this wouldn't be his last brush with James Bond and he turned out to be right about that.

Roger Moore had played a shrewd game when it came to James Bond. During the production of his TV show The Persuaders a few years before, Roger had mingled with the Bond cast and crew because they were shooting Diamonds Are Forever at the same studio. He had learned on pretty good authority that Connery definitely wasn't coming back and that the part of Bond would be up for grabs in the next film. When he heard this, Moore declined Lew Grade's offer to sign up for another series of The Persuaders so that he would be available for James Bond. Roger was 44 during the Live and Let Die casting circus. This would definitely be his last chance of playing Bond because he would be too old the next time it came around.

There seems to be some evidence that Cubby Broccoli and Harry Saltzman were not entirely convinced by Roger Moore and would have preferred Michael Billington to be cast as Bond in Live and Let Die. The story goes that United Artists disagreed. They did not want another unknown actor and so voted for Moore over Billington. The director Guy Hamilton was given the deciding vote and he too preferred Roger over Michael Billington. In the end the casting of Roger Moore made a lot of sense. He was an experienced actor and reasonably famous already because of his stint playing Simon Templar on television. Roger Moore was a safe pair of hands at a time when the franchise faced an uncertain future and couldn't really afford to take too many risks.

Roger Moore signed a three film contract and later admitted that he suspected the Bond franchise was nearing its end and that he might not even get to a third film. It has been alleged that Michael Billington was also 'retained' on an unofficial sort of contract in case they needed a new Bond again sooner than expected. Roger was the oldest actor to win the role of James Bond but - strangely enough - in Live and Let Die he could pass for the youngest. He looks incredibly boyish and youthful in the film at times. His Bond tenure was rather like The Saint on a much bigger budget. Moore's time as Bond wasn't exactly radical but it was fun. Roger Moore went on to make seven films (a record that is unlikely to ever be broken) and proved that the Bond franchise was a perfectly viable ongoing commodity even without Sean Connery. That was no mean feat.

Live and Let Die was a restart for the series after the studio and producers finally accepted they would have to go on without Sean Connery short of kidnapping him. George Lazenby was chosen because of his physical similarities to Connery and given the tropes of the cinematic Bond (tuxedo, casinos, Dom Pérignon etc) but Roger Moore was a different kettle of fish. It was the franchise that had to change to accommodate Moore - not the other way around. Roger Moore was more lightweight than the actors who came before him but more urbane and refined. Roger Moore is not the most physical actor but he's more plausible in Live and Let Die than Connery or Lazenby as someone who would know his way around an outrageously expensive wine list or designer wardrobe.

Roger Moore proved to be an excellent custodian of the Bond series and the box-office success of The Spy Who Loved Me and Moonraker at the end of the seventies found the franchise in rude commercial health. There was a slight hiccup early on in the Moore era when The Man With The Golden Gun met with a lukewarm reception in 1974 and shortly after co-producer Harry Saltzman left the franchise because of financial difficulties and sold his stake to United Artists. The Spy Who Loved Me, destined to arrive in 1977, was seen as a make or break film for Cubby Broccoli and marked a return to the epic extravaganza Bond pictures of the sixties like Thunderball and You Only Live Twice, with incredible fantastical sets by Ken Adam and lavish photography.

The Spy Who Loved Me cost twice as much as any previous Bond and the money was on the screen. It felt like a big and ambitious film compared to many previous - and subsequent - Bond entries. This was the picture that firmly established Roger Moore as James Bond. The next entry in the franchise (Moonraker) attempted to cash in on the Star Wars craze (although, strangely, Moonraker's most common touchstone is actually Kubrick's 2001 rather than Star Wars) and took James Bond into space. While purists felt the Roger Moore films were becoming too outlandish and that the comedy was beginning to get out of control, there is no question that this approach was popular with audiences at the time.

WAITING IN THE WINGS DURING THE ROGER MOORE YEARS - BILLINGTON VERSUS WARBECK

Roger Moore completed his three film Bond contract after production ended on The Spy Who Loved Me. After this Roger's appearances as Bond were negotiated on a film by film basis. Roger and Cubby Broccoli would basically play a game of bluff with one another before each film. Roger felt he wasn't paid enough and Cubby thought he was asking for too much. Despite these divergent positions though the two always remained friends and always seemed to manage to strike a last minute deal for Roger to come back.

There was a curious subplot around the time of The Spy Who Loved Me because now that his ten year embargo on remaking Thunderball was up, Kevin McClory announced plans for his own Bond film - which was to be titled Warhead. In May 1976, Kevin McClory took out an advert in Variety in which he said that production on Warhead would begin in February 1977.McClory wrote Warhead with the thriller writer Len Deighton and none other than Sean Connery. Sean Connery was said to have found it amusing that Ian Fleming - the ultimate establishment figure - lost his court case in an English court to an Irish outsider like Kevin McClory. This is presumably one of the reasons why Connery liked McClory and was now knocking about with him writing a rival Bond film. Not only was McClory and Warhead a means for Connery to get back at Cubby Broccoli, Connery also admired McClory's plucky underdog status in the movie world.

In Kevin McClory's aborted 1977 Bond film Warhead, the story had Blofeld stealing nuclear weapons in order to blackmail the United Nations into handing over control of the world's oceans to SPECTRE. The temporary headquarters of SPECTRE in Warhead was going to be inside the Statue of Liberty. There's a curious contradiction with Sean Connery's attitude to Bond in that he always expressed his displeasure with the escalating hardware and gadgets on his own Bond films and yet when he was a story consultant on Kevin McClory's Warhead the resulting story treatment was very fantastical and hardware heavy with robotic sharks and all manner of outlandish mayhem.

There was never any confirmation about who would have played Bond in Kevin McClory's Warhead film but it seems very unlikely that Sean Connery wouldn't have been tempted in the end. Who else could have done it? It's hard to think of any alternative (and plausible) option in 1977 who would have had the stature of Connery. The only people with the stature of Connery would have been Hollywood stars like Clint Eastwood and Robert Redford and they definitely wouldn't have been interested.

Cubby Broccoli naturally threw every legal obstacle at his disposal at Warhead to block McClory's film. McClory in turn took legal action over EON using SPECTRE in their movies. McClory argued (and not unreasonably too) that SPECTRE was a creation of the movie script he had written with Fleming all those years ago. The resulting legal quagmire not only torpedoed any plans EON had to use Blofeld in The Spy Who Loved Me but also any chances of Warhead going into production. In the end Sean Connery got tired of the legal wrangles and walked away. For now at least, Kevin McClory had been thwarted in his unofficial Bond ambitions.

Though Roger Moore was no spring chicken in the last phase of his tenure as Bond he was popular with audiences (ignore lazy retrospective articles which try and tell you that Roger Moore was hopeless as Bond - he was terrific and impossibly made the part his own after Connery) and pleasant and professional to work with. For this reason EON were always reluctant to part company with Roger. There were though, given Roger's age and film by film arrangement, plenty of potential Bonds waiting in the wings during his era in case he didn't come back. In fact, Cubby would often openly test actors as a way to put pressure on Roger to make a decision.

The suave English actor Michael York wrote in his autobiography that after the financial success of the 1976 sci-fi film Logan's Run he was approached by Cubby Broccoli and asked if he would be interested in playing James Bond. York said that while he was flattered he didn't think he was right for Bond. It appears that Cubby was sounding out potential Bond candidates from the late seventies onwards lest his film by film arrangement with Roger Moore should run into obstacles. York was in his early thirties and a pretty big star at the time. He had recently played D'Artagnan in Richard Lester's films The Three Musketeers and The Four Musketeers. York was a reasonable candidate although he might have been a little too posh and heritage for the role.

Was Michael Petrovitch a vague Bond candidate in the seventies? It appears that he was. Petrovitch was born in 1945 and a suavely sinister looking actor who scrubbed up well in a tux. His first credits were in Department S and Jason King. Petrovitch looked quite Bondian in the 1972 film Neither the Sea Nor the Sand and the 1973 compendium horror Tales That Witness Madness. He later appeared in television shows like Poldark and The Professionals. Petrovitch moved to Australia for a time and appeared in an eclectic stew of Aussie projects spanning from the cosy soap A Country Practice to the violent Ozploitation film Turkey Shoot. Petrovitch was someone that EON noticed but he doesn't ever appear to have been a serious candidate. On the evidence of Turkey Shoot, Petrovitch didn't age very well and by the 1980s had already lost the suave looks that won him parts in the early seventies.

Martin Shaw, who played Doyle in the popular action TV show The Professionals, has said he was invited to become a James Bond candidate in the late seventies. Shaw would have been in his early thirties at the time. "They asked me way back to do a screen test for James Bond," said Shaw. "I said no. I just didn't want to play him because it dominates everything you've done or go on to do. I was having dinner with the daughter of Cubby Broccoli. This was about 1978. She'd seen me in The Professionals and begged me to do a screen test. She was astonished when I said no thanks. Although, in retrospect, it might have been a good idea to have had a go at it."

Martin Shaw feels like a less obvious Bond candidate than his Professionals co-star Lewis Collins. While he was a good actor and quite good looking, Shaw was more of a television actor (he has done very few films) and there is no evidence that he had the charisma and presence to carry a movie. At least with Lewis Collins we have Who Dares Wins and those German/Italian action films he made as evidence that he could headline an action flick. Shaw was also one of those people who looked better when they got older. Martin Shaw was very handsome with silver hair when he became mature but he could sometimes still look a little goofy at times when he was younger. Martin Shaw's fate was to be typecast as policemen on television but he's had a great career nonetheless with plenty of impressive stage work too.

Patrick Mower claims that after Roger's third Bond (The Spy Who Loved Me) he was brought in to do an audition because Cubby wasn't sure that Roger would be back. "They thought he was too old to do another three films and he hadn't signed his contract," said Mower. "So they tested me again. But then Roger signed his contract." Around this time Mower was appearing in the cheapjack and largely forgotten police television show Target. He would have loved nothing more than to land James Bond.

Michael Billington was still very much in the loop. Billington had played a small role (as the doomed Soviet agent Sergei) in the PTS of The Spy Who Loved Me. Billington's role as Sergei is the closest we ever got to seeing him as Bond - although he said that he did not play the character in the same way he would have played 007. "I knew that if I did it, it might prevent me from doing Bond in the long run," said Billington, "but I thought "Why not?" A couple of weeks skiing and Bond was only a picture or two from demise anyway, or so I thought, "What did I care?" My choice was should I try and play it like Bond? I decided to go the anti hero route, darker inside." Billington actually looks a lot like George Lazenby in the The Spy Who Loved Me PTS! He definitely had a very Bondian sort of look with the right toupee.

When EON were testing actresses for 1979's Moonraker, Michael Billington was brought in to play Bond in the auditions against prospective leading ladies. Billington said that after the auditions, the director Lewis Gilbert told him he could and should play Bond in the next picture. Billington was invited to dinner with Cubby Broccoli after the auditions and became close to Cubby's young daughter Barbara. It seemed that Michael Billington was still very much in pole position to be the next Bond. He was essentially sitting on the substitutes bench waiting to be called onto the pitch at any moment. Billington's chances though were contingent on Roger Moore standing down sooner rather than later. Billington was nearly forty now and wasn't going to be a Bond candidate forever.

It was at the end of the seventies when Timothy Dalton got another brush with potential Bondage (if you'll pardon the expression). He was in his early thirties at the time. Dalton now seemed to be very much on the radar of Cubby Broccoli. Broccoli always kept a close eye on the male acting pool in Britain lest he should need a new Bond again. Truth be told though, Cubby was naturally a loyal and conservative man when it came to casting. The Bond films were doing perfectly well at the box-office with Roger so Cubby saw no reason to make a change if he could avoid it. When there was a mild uncertainty over Roger Moore's future participation in the franchise after Moonraker, it appears that Timothy Dalton was someone that Cubby Broccoli had on his list of potential replacements. However, Dalton was apparently not that enthused by the prospect at the time.

"There was a time in the late 1970s," Dalton later confessed in the book The Incredible World of 007, "when Roger may not have done another one, for whatever reason. They were looking around then, and I went to see Mr Broccoli in Los Angeles. At that time, they didn't have a script finished and also, the way the Bond movies had gone - although they were fun and entertaining - wasn't my idea of Bond movies. They had become a completely different entity. I know Roger, and think he does a fantastic job. He was brilliant. Roger is one of the only people in the world who can be fun in the midst of all that gadgetry. But the movies had gone a long way from their roots; they had drifted in a way that was chalk and cheese to Sean. But in truth my favorite Bond movies were always the first three."

Timothy Dalton had spent the seventies working on the stage and modestly carving out a career in film and television. Strangely though, despite his dashing good looks and acting chops, Dalton never really threatened to become a star in the seventies. He appeared in Play For today, a Dirk Bogarde espionage caper called Permission To Kill, and an obscure Spanish film called The Man Who Knew Love. By the end of the decade, Timothy Dalton's screen career seemed to be going no where in particular. He infamously appeared in the eccentric Mae West megabomb musical comedy Sextette. His other roles included the TV miniseries Centennial and Dalton also appeared in the popular TV show Charlie's Angels as the dashing Damien Roth. The one bright spot was Agatha - a decently reviewed 1979 drama about Agatha Christie's famous 11-day disappearance in 1926. Dalton played Archie Christie in a cast that included Dustin Hoffman and Vanessa Redgrave.

After the release of Moonraker in 1979, there was a lot of doubt in the entertainment world that Roger Moore would be back for a fifth film. Roger himself seemed to cast doubt on his participation in the next picture. Roger was in his fifties now and although Moonraker was a big financial success there was a sense that the franchise could do with a slight course correction and come back down to earth somewhat. The most logical way to do this was cast a new actor and begin a new era. This is essentially what EON planned to do at the time. In 1980, EON brought David Warbeck back for a three day screen test. Warbeck was 39 years-old and at the start of his Italian horror and 'Macaroni Combat' phase. Warbeck would become something of a cult B-movie horror and action star in Italy. In the Billington v Warbeck battle of the reserve Bonds it appears there was a very brief window in time here where Warbeck edged his nose in front.

According to David Warbeck, he was selected to play Bond in the next picture and John Hough (director of films such as The Legend of Hell House and Escape to Witch Mountain) was to direct. "I can't recall what titles they were," said Hough. "What happened was that Roger Moore had entered into dispute with Cubby Broccoli over salary and this was something that was documented in Variety and the trade papers and Roger was looking for a hike in pay, and so, had decided that he wouldn't play Bond again unless he was paid an increase in salary. At this point the Bond company had decided they wouldn't do that and they would go with a new James Bond and a new director. They choose an actor called David Warbeck who was secretly tested. I had directed David Warbeck in a film called Wolfshead (aka Wolfshead: The Legend of Robin Hood), which is a very highly regarded little film.

"Cubby Broccoli had seen this and had decided that if David Warbeck got to play James Bond then I would get to direct Bonds. In fact, they did a two picture deal with me because they were going to do two James Bonds, back-to-back. The idea was, at that particular point, they wouldn't do just one James Bond at time but we were going to do two at a time. And so, two directors would both alternate and do a Bond each and the whole thing was pretty much set up. But before David Warbeck got the chance to sign the contract, Roger Moore had decided that he would go ahead and take the deal that was on the table. I knew that he and I would never work together because we had a dispute on the Saint TV series and we weren't compatible. The chance never arose past that point."

The Hough/Warbeck concept is sort of confusing in that Warbeck's test was directed by John Glen - who ended up directing the next film. Were Hough and Glen supposed to alternate on directing Bond films? David Warbeck said his proposed Bond film was nixed by a financial crash. This could be a reference to the failure of Heaven's Gate proving to be a box-office disaster for United Artists in 1980. In his memoir, Cubby Broccoli said that United Artists were very pro-Roger Moore when it came to the James Bond franchise in the early 80s. They felt that Roger was popular and established in the role and saw no need to make a change for the time being.

Of his 1980 Bond audition, Warbeck said - "It's ironic that I was actually contracted to be the new Bond and my director was going to be Johnny Hough, because I had chats with Broccoli and said no, I didn't want to work with John Glen, because I have this problem with directors. John Glen and Martin Campbell, well the younger Martin Campbell were sort of similar in that they just didn't share my sense of humour and my sense of humour is based on experience and it's based on visual gags. For example, when I did the Bond bits with John Glen, there was a sequence where somebody sticks a gun in my back while I'm on the telephone and I thought it would be a great visual gag if when he says "put your hands up" you've still got the telephone in your hand with the cord attached. And so you whack him with the telephone and then you try to strangle him with the cord while the person on the other end is still talking! You see what I mean? It would have been a good visual as well as well as plot gag, but John Glen wouldn't see that."

David Warbeck said that his extensive screen test was at Pinewood with elaborate security. It was all very hush hush. The odd thing about Warbeck becoming the new Bond at that time is that his career was floundering somewhat and he still wasn't very well known - although of course Bond actors tend not to be tremendously famous when they are cast. EON have never cast an A'list star as Bond and probably never will. It actually tends to help if the new Bond actor isn't that well known because then it's easier for the audience to simply accept them as Bond. This is why, to give an example, many believe that Henry Cavill's future Bond hopes became more remote when he was cast as Superman.

Around the time of his Bond screen test for John Glen, Warbeck had just appeared in a film called The Last Hunter (L'ultimo cacciatore). The Last Hunter is a sort of bargain basement Italian blend of The Deer Hunter and Rambo (though it of course pre-dates the Rambo films) and has Warbeck as Captain Henry Morris - a soldier who goes on a deadly mission behind enemy lines during the Vietnam War. Warbeck is actually quite a commanding and macho presence in this blood drenched nonsense though he does seem to be losing his hair so one suspects that a Connery style toupee might have been put on order had he got the 007 gig. Warbeck is also very thin and looks like he could do with a bit of gym time and a few square meals.

Warbeck was in the cult horror film The Beyond in 1981 and then made Hunters of the Golden Cobra. Hunters of the Golden Cobra is a cheapjack Italian version of Raiders of the Lost Ark and Warbeck is actually quite James Bondish in this. His acting style is a sort of likeable mix of Roger Moore and Lewis Collins and Warbeck does look the part of 007 - especially when he is clad in an all black outfit of the type that Roger Moore had on near the end of Live and Let Die. Warbeck was also rather James Bondish in the 1982 Italian action film Tiger Joe and 1984's The Ark of the Sun God (another low-budget Italian riff on Indiana Jones).

In 1984, Warbeck was in an episode of the popular British drama show Minder and played a snooty man who crosses swords with George Cole's Arthur Daley over some antique furniture. This episode of Minder showed that Warbeck was certainly refined and suave enough to be Bond - although by 1984 his 007 dream was fading fast. Warbeck usually imbued his characters with a tongue-in-cheek sort of humour and no doubt would have done this had he played Bond. You could maybe argue then that Warbeck perhaps wouldn't have been a big enough departure from Roger Moore. Warbeck's Bond definitely would have been funny but was this really what the series needed at the time? To be fair to Warbeck though he was capable too of bringing a certain world weariness to his characters.

The next Bond film was of course settled as For Your Eyes Only with John Glen in the director's chair for the first time. Glen said that they tested numerous actors because they presumed Roger wasn't coming back. "To be honest I did want to make another film," said Roger Moore of this uncertain period. "This was all part of the bargaining ploy on EON's side - let it be known they were testing others so I'd take the deal on the table for fear of losing the part. Fair enough, we all enjoy a game of poker. I'm quite principled about not undervaluing my worth. If someone wants me for a job then I believe they should pay me a fair fee. My agent usually haggles it up a bit, the producer usually haggles it down a bit and a happy middle ground is found. If someone undervalues me, I simply walk away. I have no qualms about it."

One actor who EON cast their eye over during this period is Nicholas Clay. His most notable role was around this time was as Lancelot in John Boorman's Excalibur. It could be that Clay was looked at after this film came out - which would mean he was considered for Octopussy rather than For Your Eyes Only. Clay was very handsome and very posh. He looked the part but you wouldn't say he was the most natural actor in the world. I shall forever remember Nicholas Clay for a fascinatingly bizarre episode of Hammer House of Mystery & Suspense where he plays a man who finds himself trapped in his house with his family when a mysterious and impenetrable wall suddenly encloses their home! Around this time Clay also made the enjoyable Agatha Christie adaptation Evil Under the Sun for director Guy Hamilton.

Anthony Andrews is often cited as someone who EON looked

at for Bond in the eighties. This is hard to verify as Andrews has never mentioned it himself. Besides, Andrews was someone who tended to prefer the stage to films or commercial projects. Andrews turned down the lead role in the 1982-1987 TV show Remington Steele because he didn't want to move his family to Hollywood. He was replaced by a young unknown actor called Pierce Brosnan. One other notable thing about Andrews is that he was originally cast as Bodie in the TV show The Professionals but fired after four days because he wasn't tough enough and too similar to Martin Shaw (who played Doyle). Andrews was of course replaced by Lewis Collins. Though he is a very good actor, Andrews feels too light to have been Bond. You can't really see him beating people up with cinematic verisimilitude.

Michael Jayston has claimed that he was one of the actors who was lined up to replace Roger Moore in For Your Eyes Only. Jayston had recently appeared in the TV miniseries Tinker Tailor Soldier Spy. His film roles included Cromwell, Tales That Witness Madness, and Zulu Dawn. Jayston was 45 though so rather knocking on a bit to be making his Bond debut. Though a crisp and polished actor, Jayston wasn't the most screamingly Bondian actor in terms of looks. Jayston would have been a more credible 007 candidate in the early seventies rather than the early eighties. Interestingly, Jayston claimed that one of the actors he was competing with for the part of Bond in For Your Eyes Only was Patrick Mower. If true, this would surely rank Mower up there with Warbeck and Billington when it came to enduring and perennial Bond candidates! Mower was now in his early forties and about to shoot a part in the detective series Bergerac.

When they began pre-production on For Your Eyes Only, stuntmen with black hair were hired because they assumed they were getting a new Bond actor. When Roger came back at the last minute they had to let the black-haired stuntmen go and replace them with fair-haired ones! Because it was not known if Roger Moore was coming back, For Your Eyes Only was written in a rather generic way when it came to James

Bond in the film. The opening scene where Bond places flowers on his wife's grave was written to connect a new Bond actor to the history of the franchise. Although the game of bluff over Roger's salary became a familiar preamble to each new Bond film it does appear as if went down to the wire on For Your Eyes Only. We could very nearly have had a new Bond actor on that film.

The actor who came the closest to becoming the new Bond in For Your Eyes Only was (no great surprise here) Michael Billington. Billington was still very much in the loop and still close to the Broccoli family. Michael Billington was flown to Corfu lest Roger should not return. He was put in a tux (and later a black polo neck) and given a Bondian photo shoot. Billington still looked good and would have made a credible and competent Bond had they needed a fresh last minute 007.

"Time passed and For Your Eyes Only was on the horizon," said Billington. "By this time the 'usual suspects' were gone. John Glen was at the helm; script by Richard Maibaum, close to retirement and Michael G. Wilson, a lawyer by profession. The sharp and witty Christopher Woods dialogue was sadly no more. The troops were gathering to go to Corfu to begin filming but Roger was being coy. I think the money was an issue. Cubby had me fitted out with wardrobe and flew me to Corfu. We had a picture shoot." Once again, Roger Moore decided to come back and Billington wasn't required in the end. Billington's enthusiasm for Bond, if his website (where he shared his memories of his acting career and brush with Bond fame) is anything to go by, seemed to be on the wane by this point. He said he didn't like For Your Eyes Only very much when he watched it.

One of the cast members of For Your Eyes Only was the Australian actress Cassandra Harris as Countess Lisl von Schlaf. Harris had recently got married to a young Irish actor named Pierce Brosnan. At the time, Brosnan's credits only amounted to small roles in The Long Good Friday and The Mirror Crack'd. During the production of the film, Cassandra

Harris introduced Brosnan to Cubby Broccoli and Broccoli immediately made a mental note of Brosnan as a potential future Bond. Brosnan was dark haired, tall, very handsome, and very charming. Cubby thought that if Brosnan could polish up his acting skills he'd make a perfect James Bond in the not too distant future.

After the release of For Your Eyes Only in 1981 there was again doubt that Roger would be back for the next film. Roger was 53 and would be 55 by the time the next film came out. Once again the familiar game of poker over Roger's fee led to more Bond auditions and interviews. These interviews included a very obvious candidate - Lewis Collins. To people in Britain at least, Lewis Collins was the James Bond that got away. It's impossible to watch The Professionals or the 1982 action film Who Dares Wins and not think that Collins would have made a terrific Bond. Collins is believed to have had a meeting with Cubby Broccoli circa 1982. He was in his mid thirties at the time.

Collins was tough, sardonic, and good at action and fights. He was a little on the short side but he had black hair and a good look for Bond. Lewis Collins would have brought the franchise back to earth and played a tougher sort of Bond but he was good with humour too and always seemed to layer a self-deprecation into his characters. "I think it is time for a change, although no one has approached me," said Lewis Collins of James Bond in the early eighties. "What I would be interested in is a new character, starting from scratch - an Eighties version of Bond, getting away from the gadgets a bit. When Connery started you really believed he could kill someone with his bare hands. He was an animal, but a smooth one. Since then, Bond has been watered down. I think what the Bond films need is a more gripping storyline. The public needs to be more involved with the character. You need a human being the public cares about."

Lewis Collins had signed a three film contract with producer Euan Lloyd which was projected to make Collins a big star.

"He's a strong actor with a lot of charisma and I'm sure that
with a major campaign behind him he will become a big star,"
said Lloyd. Things didn't quite go according to plan though.
Who Dares Wins (in which Collins plays an SAS captain who
foils an embassy siege) was completed but the second
proposed film, Wild Geese 2, saw Collins replaced by Scott
Glenn. The third film in the Collins/Lloyd contract was
supposed to be an action drama about the Falklands War but
this film never got made. As a consequence of all of this Lewis
Collins never became a movie star.

Although he seemed like an obvious person to replace Roger
Moore the Bond dream of Lewis Collins proved frustratingly
elusive. What sunk his prospects was the fact that Cubby
Broccoli seemed to take an instant dislike to him when they
met. "I was in Cubby Broccoli's office for five minutes," said
Collins, "but it was really over for me in seconds. I have heard
since that he doesn't like me. That's unfair. He's expecting
another Connery to walk through the door and there are few of
them around. I think he's really shut the door on me. He found
me too aggressive. I knew it all -- that kind of attitude. Two or
three years ago that would be the case, purely because I was
nervous and defensive. I felt they were playing the producer
bit with fat cigars. When someone walks into their office for
the most popular film job in the world, a little actor is bound
to put on a few airs. If Cubby couldn't see I was being self-
protective I don't have faith in his judgment. It would be nice
to get back to the original Bond, not the character created by
Sean Connery - but the one from the books. He's not over-
handsome, over-tall. He's about my age and has got my
attitudes."

Brian Clemens, creator of The Professionals, said of Lewis
Collins - "I thought he would have made a marvellous Bond.
He was tough and he could fight, he looked good, he was
handsome and he had this nice sense of humour. I knew he
had auditioned [for James Bond] and I think they were wrong
not to take him up. He took up parachute jumping soon after
joining The Professionals. It was the sort of thing you would

expect a Marine to indulge in. He was a method actor in a sense." After his disastrous interview with Cubby Broccoli, Lewis Collins thanked the British public for their support in touting him for the Bond role and said he hoped he'd get another shot at bagging the part.

The next Bond film was 1983's Octopussy. Once again an air of uncertainty hung in the air regarding Roger Moore's participation. The person who came closest to being cast as Roger's replacement this time was not Michael Billington but the American actor James Brolin. Brolin was 43 and had appeared in films like The Amityville Horror and Westworld. He was 6'4, handsome, and suave. Brolin did an extensive screen test with Octopussy stars Maud Adams and Vijay Amritraj and at one point was very close to signing on the dotted line. You could say that Brolin was sort of like the 1980s version of John Gavin when it came to Bond. Close but no cigar.

Brolin did his audition in an American accent because they simply wanted to get a feel for how Brolin looked and how he would play a Bondian sort of scene. He would obviously have had to have worked on an English accent later. Brolin looks terrific in his screen test although he is a trifle wooden. Whether he would have made a good Bond is open to question but there's no doubt he would have looked good in a tux. There is evidence that Brolin was a candidate for For Your Eyes Only and first came on the radar of EON after the film Capricorn One in 1978. John Glen, who directed Brolin's Bond auditions, said that testing Brolin was a tactic designed to put pressure on Roger Moore to accept terms for Octopussy. Cubby Broccoli even toyed with the idea of offering Superman star Christopher Reeve the part of James Bond in an effort to jolt Roger into signing a contract.

Oliver Tobias also auditioned to play Bond in Octopussy. The Swiss born actor was about 35 at the time. His film roles included Arabian Adventure and The Stud. The Stud made Tobias something of a sex symbol at the time. He never really became a film star but he did have a solid career with plenty of good television work. Tobias, like Brolin, did a fight scene at Pinewood as part of his test. Another actor who auditioned for Bond in the eighties was Steve Adler. Adler, who was born in 1950, played Murphy in The Professionals. Adler was tall and good looking but whether he had the right look for Bond is debatable. His last screen credit was in The Bill in 1994 and he sadly died three years later.

Daniel Pilon, who was interviewed for OHMSS, claims that he was approached again in the early eighties about playing 007 - which is slightly odd because it was the long departed Harry Saltzman who was his advocate rather than Cubby Broccoli. It has been alleged that Ben Cross was someone who EON had their eye on as a potential Bond at this time. Cross was still in his thirties and sprang to prominence as a member of the Royal Shakespeare Company. In 1981 he portrayed the athlete Harold Abrahams in the Oscar winning film Chariots of Fire. Cross doesn't seem like an unreasonable Bond candidate in terms of his looks and was obviously a very good actor but whether he would actually have been interested in the part at the time is another matter.

Still in contention was Michael Billington. This would be the last time though that Billington was a Bond candidate. His time had nearly run out. Billington had moved to the United States at this time to enhance his acting career but he didn't have much luck. Billington was cast as Count Louis Dardinay in an action adventure show called The Quest produced by Stephen J. Cannell but The Quest was cancelled after five episodes in 1982. If you look on YouTube you can watch the pilot episode for The Quest and it's clear from this pilot that Billington was still more than capable of playing Bond. He is crisp and commanding and still looks the part. A couple of years later Billington appeared in the television movie Antony and Cleopatra. One of his co-stars was a certain Timothy Dalton.

"Octopussy rolled around. Roger this time was being extra

coy," said Billington. "I tested once more with Deborah Sheldon and Susan Penhaligon but it was purely cosmetic. I didn't feel John Glenn was truly an actors director. And anyway he seemed more secure with Roger so, in my view; he needed me and any other candidate for that matter, like acute pneumonia. And with all respect, Michael G Wilson was not really a writer. And, with all the will in the world, I couldn't quite see myself dressed as a circus clown clutching a Faberge Egg and the finale with the ticking time bomb was in my view a resurrected dead turkey, so consequently I was uncharacteristically very, very nervous of the prospects."

In the end Roger Moore returned to make Octopussy. One of the main reasons why they wanted Roger back was the release of the unofficial Bond film Never Say Never Again with Sean Connery in 1983. EON wanted an established Bond rather than a new actor to go up against Connery. In the end they needn't have worried. An agreement was reached for the films to be released at different times. Octopussy made more money in the end than Never Say Never Again - which obviously seemed to justify the decision to get Roger back. Despite all the Battle of the Bonds headlines, Roger Moore and Sean Connery remained friends and even had dinner a few times while these films were in production. Curiously, it was later revealed that Kevin McClory had planned two remakes of Thunderball at this time and wanted Magnum star Tom Selleck to play Bond in the second film. This obviously didn't happen in the end. It was a bit of a pipedream to imagine he could make two versions of Thunderball - let alone persuade Tom Selleck to play James Bond.

Dick Clement and Ian La Frenais, two legendary British sitcom writers, were hired by Sean Connery to polish the script for Never Say Never Again. Clement and La Frenais's script had the opening to the movie (where Connery's Bond is infiltrating a jungle mansion) playing out against the backdrop of a ticking clock to make it tense and exciting. Clement and La Frenais were mortified when they watched the film and saw that the exciting opening sequence now had Lani Hall's soppy theme song over it rather than a ticking clock. According to Dick Clement and Ian La Frenais, the script and production of Never Say Never Again was so amateurish that the crew started shooting scenes in the Bahamas without the script having any explanation whatsoever for why Bond should be in the Bahamas! They had to add an explanation into the script.

Irvin Kershner, the director of Never Say Never Again, said that many planned sequences either had to be scrapped or scaled down because of the lack of money. He felt as if he always had one arm tied behind his back on that movie and that it could have been much better with a bigger budget. Never Say Never Again was supposed to begin with a sequence at a medieval pageant where one knight is killed in a jousting display. A third knight gives chase on horseback and is revealed to be 007. This sequence was never shot because they didn't have the time nor the money. Sean Connery's renegade Bond film Never Say Never Again was produced by Jack Schwartzman. Jack Schwartzman was so terrified of Sean Connery he tried to avoid him on the set (which obviously couldn't have been an easy task). Connery, never one to suffer fools, thought that Schwartzman was incompetent and so the relationship between the men was difficult to say the least. Schwartzman had to dip into his own pocket to get Never Say Never Again finished when the film ran over its budget.

Every fresh script rewrite on Never Say Never Again had to be approved by an insurance company lest it should flout Kevin McClory's strictly defined Bond rights (which permitted to remake Thunderball - NOT make up his own Bond film) and give Cubby Broccoli any fresh legal ammunition. Right up until the week that Never Say Never Again was due to hit cinemas, Cubby Broccoli and EON were still in court trying to block the film's release. Max Von Sydow played Blofeld in Never Say Never Again but most of his scenes ended up on the cutting room floor - to the point where it seemed pointless to have hired him the first place! Although most Bond fans would probably agree that Never Say Never Again could have been a lot better, it got incredible reviews when it first came out. The

Chicago Sun Times likened the return of Connery to a Beatles reunion. Never Say Never Again grossed $160 million from a $36 million budget. In the 1990s there were stories that a new version of Never Say Never Again was going to be released on laserdisc with a new music score and much deleted footage put back in. Most Bond fans would pay money to watch that.

US Magazine asked its readers in 1983 to vote for who they thought the next Bond should be. The poll was won by Pierce Brosnan in a landslide with 46% of the vote. In second place with 11% was Lewis Collins. Other names who earned votes from readers were Tom Selleck, Ian Oglivy, and Mel Gibson. In the preamble to A View To A Kill going into production there were vague rumours that Lewis Collins was back in contention but these turned out not to have much basis in fact.

"I really don't know if I am in the running," said Lewis Collins in 1984. "I certainly haven't been approached by Broccoli. If they did approach me, I don't know what I would say – it really would depend on what was offered. If I had to sign a seven-year contract I'd probably say 'No' just because I wouldn't want to be that tied down. I certainly wouldn't envy anyone taking over the role at this stage, especially if they kept to the same format. They would have to allow the next guy to be himself and bring what he has to offer to the role. And then, it would take at least two movies to convince the world you are Bond. Even so, I have to admit it would be fun."

From 1984 to 1988, Lewis Collins made a trilogy of Italian/German action films for the director Antonio Margheriti. Margheriti had directed David Warbeck in his Euro action capers so Collins was basically stepping into Warbeck's shoes. The films were Code Name: Wild Geese, Commando Leopard, and The Commander. These movies are undemanding fun with co-stars like Lee Van Cleef, Klaus Kinski and Ernest Borgnine. Lewis Collins said he didn't like these movies much and only did them for the money. He was tiring of being typecast as an action man and wanted to do other things. Many sources contend that Collins was in the mix for The Living Daylights (he was only 40 so still young enough) in 1986 but his Bond dream never came close to happening. One can't help thinking that Lewis Collins would have been a fun eighties Bond. Imagine Bodie from The Professionals with a better haircut. You've pretty much got 007 right there!

Roger Moore would go to appear in A View To A Kill in 1985 before finally bowing out of the Bond franchise. He was 57 and it was time to make way for a new actor. 1984, the year before Roger Moore's last Bond film was released, saw a number of rumours that Pierce Brosnan was going to be the new Bond. An Australian newspaper published an article in which they said Brosnan had already signed a secret deal to replace Roger. Brosnan had to deny these rumours and even wrote to Cubby Broccoli assuring him that these stories did not originate from him or anyone connected to him. It was pretty obvious though that Pierce Brosnan was now in pole position. People watched his TV show Remington Steele and couldn't help but imagine him as James Bond. The part suddenly seemed to be Brosnan's to lose now.

* John Hough and Roger Moore had fallen out years before when Hough directed an episode of The Saint. Hough said that on one scene he made Roger do fourteen takes and Roger was absolutely furious because he hated doing multiple takes and sort of resented this young director trying to boss him around on his own show. After this experience Roger was in no hurry to ever work with John Hough again. There was probably little chance of Roger agreeing to do a Bond film if Hough was directing.

THE LIVING DAYLIGHTS

1987 would mark the 25th anniversary of the James Bond series and what better way to celebrate than to launch a new era which looked to the future? The Bond producer Michael G

Wilson felt that the series needed to make some radical changes to stay fresh and relevant after seven Roger Moore films. Wilson drafted a treatment which was essentially an origin story. Wilson's script treatment had a twentysomething Bond teaming up with a veteran agent to battle a Chinese warlord named Kwang. By the end of the story, the veteran agent is dead and Bond has inherited his mantle and become a full fledged secret agent. The story would show us how Bond met M, Q and Moneypenny for the first time.

According to CinemaBlend, this treatment '... would have introduced the world to Lieutenant James Bond as he lives a carefree youth of punching out Austrian diplomats and gambling away what's left of his family fortune. Bond's grandfather and aunt are introduced at the Bond family's ancestral home, with James deciding to take up M's invitation into her majesty's secret service after his grandfather's passing. Learning from his mentor, 00-agent Bart Trevor, we eventually learn that Trevor recruited Bond into a mission to kidnap/kill a warlord known as General Kwang required someone with his skills on a short notice.'

The reboot story would have seen Bond travel to Scotland to explore his roots (something which EON clearly put in the bank and used for Skyfall) and end with him being asked to investigate Dr No. A DC3 aeroplane sequence in the treatment later seemed to end up in the 2008 film Quantum of Solace. It is pretty obvious that this treatment, had it gone ahead, would not have featured Timothy Dalton - who was nearly 40 at the time. This story would obviously have required a Bond actor in his twenties.

Michael G Wilson's reboot script treatment (which was obviously an influence on Casino Royale in 2006 - though Wilson has downplayed this connection himself) was vetoed by Cubby Broccoli in the end. Cubby felt that audiences would not want to see James Bond depicted as a youthful amateur. He wasn't sold on the idea at all and preferred a more business as usual approach where Bond is a mature professional in his thirties or forties. Cubby was though willing to accept that changes would have to be made to the franchise to keep it fresh. He wanted the next film to be more grounded and feel like more of a blood relative to Ian Fleming than many of Roger Moore films had been.

It was decided that the next film would be called The Living Daylights. The Living Daylights took its title from Octopussy and The Living Daylights - the fourteenth and final James Bond book by Ian Fleming and published posthumously in 1966. There are four stories in this slim volume - two of which were added in later additions. The first two stories (Octopussy and the Property of a Lady) contained some elements which were used in the 1983 Roger Moore film Octopussy.

Octopussy concerns a murder victim called Hans Oberhauser who is found frozen in an Austrian glacier. James Bond is sent to Jamaica to talk to the last man to see the victim before his death. This just happens to be a certain Major Dexter Smythe. Bond is personally involved in the case as Oberhauser was a mentor to him in his younger days after the death of his parents. This short story was also an influence on the controversial Blofeld twist in the Daniel Craig film Spectre. The last story in the collection is 007 in New York. 007 in New York is a mildly interesting trifle that consists of Bond's general musings about New York and also a lot about food and where he will go to eat.

It was the third story that inspired the title and some elements for 1987's The Living Daylights. In this story a British agent known as '272' is heading back to the West through Berlin and the Soviets are sending their top assassin - codenamed 'Trigger' - to shoot him as he makes his way across no-man's land. M sends James Bond to kill the KGB assassin and 007 hunkers down in a safe house with his sniper rifle waiting for a shot at his target. What appears to be a female orchestra go in and out of the building Bond is keeping watch on.

Ian Fleming's The Living Daylights revolves around Bond's

distaste for killing - despite it often being an unavoidable part of his job. This story would be incorporated into the beginning of the 1987 Timothy Dalton film of the same name in faithful fashion and presents us with a more weary, tired Bond who is questioning his profession and the things he has to do in the name of Queen and Country. There is a decent twist in Fleming's story when the target is revealed and the main drama comes from Bond's reaction to what he has been asked to do.

It is sometimes reported that The Living Daylights was originally written for Roger Moore but this was not the case. Richard Maibaum and Wilson knew that a new actor would be coming in for the next film. The identity of that actor proved in the end to be a rather complex and circuitous puzzle to solve though. There was something of a changing of the guard this time round when it came to Bond candidates. David Warbeck and Michael Billington were both now 45 and had finally aged out of contention. These two had been around since OHMSS and were basically duking it out to be the next Bond in the early eighties but their 007 window had finally closed for good.

David Warbeck continued to make films in Italy and embraced the cultish status he eventually attained for his various roles in these fun low-budget pictures. His last credit was a horror movie called Razor Blade Smile. David Warbeck sadly died of cancer in 1998. He was only 55 years-old. Michael Billington seemed to struggle to find work in the end. His last credit was as a villain in a 1993 episode of Maigret. Billington did though enjoy plenty of cultish fame for his role in Gerry Anderson's UFO and appeared at many fan events and conventions. He died in 2005 at the age of 67. With the exception of John Gavin, Michael Billington was the actor who came closest to the part without actually getting to play James Bond. This is rather a shame as I think Michael Billington could have been a very good James Bond.

Cubby Broccoli thought he had solved the latest pesky James Bond casting riddle when Pierce Brosnan (who was about 33

at the time) officially signed on to play 007 in The Living
Daylights. Brosnan's casting felt like a no brainer. Cubby had
obviously not forgotten meeting Brosnan on the set of For
Your Eyes Only and kept tabs on him. Brosnan had begun his
007 costume fittings and shot a gunbarrel intro for The Living
Daylights when fate intervened in very cruel fashion.

Brosnan's NBC (and produced by MTM Enterprises) television
show Remington Steele - a piece of eighties fluff that had
Brosnan as a suave pseudo private eye - was ailing in the
ratings and on the way out but the studio decided to cash in on
the publicity surrounding Brosnan and James Bond and
optioned a new series just as Brosnan's contract was about to
expire. NBC offered to adjust their Remington Steele
schedules so Brosnan could still do The Living Daylights but
Cubby Broccoli declined to take advantage of this offer. In
those days television had less prestige than it does today and
Broccoli simply didn't want to share his Bond actor with a TV
show.

Broccoli had apparently told NBC they could have Brosnan for
six episodes but NBC insisted on 22 episodes so no
compromise could be arranged and EON decided to move on.
"James Bond will not be Remington Steele, and Remington
Steele will not be James Bond," declared Broccoli. The
decision to 'reactivate' Remington Steele had had equally
frustrating consequences for Brosnan's co-star Stephanie
Zimbalist, who played Laura Holt in Remington Steele.
Zimbalist had been cast as Officer Lewis in Paul Verhoeven's
Robocop but had to abandon the film and go back to making
Steele with Brosnan. She was replaced in Robocop by Nancy
Allen.

"My first reaction," said Brosnan, "was to tell them to shove
the Remington contract. It was a knife in the heart. And not
just for me, for my family, because we moved our children
back to England and got ****** over by very short people.
They had me by the short and curlies and there was absolutely
nothing I could do. They'd nailed me to the wall. I went out

and played a lot of tennis - to get the anger out of my system. You get over it. It's just being an actor."

Now that a furious Pierce Brosnan was out of the picture, Cubby Broccoli (apparently on the advice of his wife Dana) turned to Timothy Dalton and offered him the part of James Bond in The Living Daylights. Broccoli had always liked Dalton and always kept note of his career. Broccoli described Dalton as - "A vanishing breed, a gentleman actor with a highly tolerable ego!" However Dalton, who was now 40 years-old, declined the part because of existing theatrical commitments (in 1986, Dalton appeared in both Antony and Cleopatra and The Taming of the Shrew). Dalton's schedule was also complicated by a Brooke Shields adventure film called Brenda Starr he had signed up to appear in.

This then was the third time that Dalton had been approached about playing Bond and the third time he had recoiled from the overtures. This time was slightly different though in that Dalton's hands were tied (this was also the first time too that he had actually been offered the part). Dalton was contracted to both a play and a movie so was simply unavailable. It was tough luck but Dalton, who was never really that interested in stardom, wasn't unduly bothered by having to turn down James Bond, certainly in comparison to Brosnan - who was crestfallen to lose the part of Bond at the last minute.

With both Pierce Brosnan and Timothy Dalton apparently out of the running, this opened the door for any number of other actors to come into contention to play James Bond in The Living Daylights. It was rather like a tennis tournament where the top two seeds have been knocked out early and so everyone now fancies their chances! The New Zealand actor Sam Neill was now the preferred choice of many at EON to become the new Bond. The television series Reilly, Ace Of Spies and a suave turn as the diabolical Damien Thorn in the trashy Omen III had made Neill a viable 007 candidate. It was arranged for him to do a screen test (as ever with Bond auditions he acted out a From Russia with Love scene) at Pinewood but Neill was atrocious in the audition and seemed disinterested. Cubby Broccoli was never really sold on Sam Neill and the dire screentest merely confirmed his opinion.

Years later, Sam Neill explained his low energy Bond audition when he said he had no interest at all in playing James Bond and had been pressured into the audition by his agent. "I don't know why I was asked to audition, but I was, and I did, against my better judgment. My agent, who has now left this mortal coil, so I suppose I can say what I like. But she was deluded about certain things, and one of her delusions was that Bond would've been good for me, and vice versa, so I went very reluctantly out to test for that. And to my great relief, I didn't get the part, and I haven't looked back. It was one of the worst days of my life. I didn't want to be there, and I was so uncomfortable all day. There was nothing good about the day at all."

Another actor who auditioned to be James Bond in 1986 was Mark Greenstreet. Greenstreet had just appeared in a miniseries called Brat Farrar and spent three days doing screen tests at Pinewood. Greenstreet later said that during a break he went to use the toilet and bumped into Michael Biehn in his Corporal Hicks colonial space marine costume (James Cameron was shooting his classic sequel Aliens at the studio while Greenstreet's auditions took place). The interesting thing about Greenstreet is that he was only 25 at the time - which suggests EON, at some point, had a vague idea about making Bond much younger than usual.

Greenstreet spoke about his James Bond test in an appearance on Terry Wogan's chat show. Greenstreet said the first scene didn't go terribly well because he trapped his finger in a door while trying to make a suave entrance! Terry Wogan also commented on Greenstreet's hair and said it would be very strange to have a blond Bond! Greenstreet seemed a trifle too foppish to be Bond and doesn't appear to have got very close to the part. Michael Praed, the star of the TV show Robin Sherwood, was another actor who tested for The Living

Daylights. Praed did his Bond audition with Fiona Fullerton. Michael Praed said he was told a month later that he had the part but this obviously didn't turn out to be the case. Around this time Praed had just finished a stint in the glossy US soap opera Dynasty. Praed was still in his twenties at the time so, like Mark Greenstreet, another very young candidate.

Another young actor who had contact with EON in 1986 was Marcus Gilbert. Gilbert was in his late twenties and dashingly handsome - not to mention blond! He had appeared in films like The Masks of Death and Biggles: Adventures in Time. It doesn't appear though that Gilbert got the full audition treatment. Gilbert's most famous role came in the 1993 Jilly Cooper television mini-series Riders - a 'sex sizzler' set in the world of show jumping. Michael Praed played Gilbert's romantic rival in Riders so you got two Bond candidates for the price of one in that project! Gilbert would later appear in some Hollywood films like Army of Darkness and Rambo III.

MGM's new chief Jerry Weintraub suggested they should break the bank and cast Mel Gibson as Bond. Gibson would later say that he turned down James Bond twice because the part didn't interest him. Tom Mankiewicz, former writer on Bond films for Cubby Broccoli, disputed this though and said it was Cubby Broccoli who didn't want Gibson and not the other way around. According to Mankicwicz, Cubby felt Gibson was too famous and they would end up making a Mel Gibson movie rather than a James Bond movie. Cubby is also alleged to have felt that the 5'9 Gibson was far too short to play James Bond. "Cubby had a thing about tall people," said Mankiewicz. "Bond had to be tall, and Mel Gibson was too short."

Patrick Mower claims to have been considered for The Living Daylights but this seems exceptionally unlikely because of his age. Why would you replace Roger with a 48 year-old Patrick Mower? What would be the point? Mower would have been too old for the part after a couple of films! It seems much more likely that Mower had joined Warbeck and Billington as a perennial former James Bond candidate who had simply aged out of contention by the end of the Roger Moore era.

The resident Bond director John Glen was quite keen on Highlander star Christopher Lambert playing Bond in The Living Daylights but Lambert's heavily accented and not exactly fluent English made this an unlikely prospect. Lambert was about 30 at the time and had appeared in films like Subway and Greystoke. Although he won critical acclaim for his French language films, Lambert always came across as rather wooden when acting in English. He was a very good looking man but it's difficult to imagine he could have made a very good James Bond. One other strike against Lambert was that he was only 5'9. Cubby definitely would have considered this too short to convincingly play Bond.

A surprising candidate for The Living Daylights was Trevor Eve. Eve was 35 and best known in Britain at the time for the TV show Shoestring - where he played a down at heel private detective who wore shabby suits and liked a moustache. Eve's most famous film role at the time was in the 1979 film Dracula. Trevor Eve was also a highly acclaimed stage actor and it is this that probably put him on the radar of EON (I can't believe anyone at EON HQ watched Shoestring and went "That's our Bond!" - it must have been Eve's stage work that caught their eye). Eve was quite a handsome and suave man away from his Shoestring image so maybe him being a Bond candidate isn't as surprising as it might sound at first glance. John Glen has said that Eve tested for Bond although Trevor Eve said he simply had a meeting with Barbara Broccoli. Eve is probably best known now for his role as Detective Superintendent Peter Boyd in BBC television drama Waking the Dead.

Bond fans used to wonder if Finlay Light was even a real person. A newspaper article in 1986 claimed he was a 32 year-old Australian model who had signed a ten year contract to become the new Bond but any evidence of Finlay Light being a real person was thin on the ground at the ground. However, while he didn't get the part he was actually real. John Glen confirmed in his memoir that Finlay Light tested for The Living Daylights. Light only had one acting credit but had somehow entered the orbit of EON and become a Bond contender. He was 6'2 and quite handsome (although he looks alarmingly like David Icke in one of the few photos of him on the web!) but Light's inexperience as an actor was obviously something that must have counted against him in the end.

The super suave Ian Ogilvy said that he was in contact with the Bond people circa 1985 but told he was too similar to Roger Moore to play the part. Ogilvy had of course replaced Moore as Simon Templar on television years before. "When they told me I wasn't going to get the part because I was too similar to Roger Moore," said Ogilvy, "I felt relieved. You have to be terribly confident as Bond and I honestly don't think I could have carried it off." Ian Ogilvy was in his early forties at the time. He actually would have been a terrific Bond candidate in the late sixties and early seventies and may well have been considered too in those eras. The Den of Geek website claimed that Ogilvy was also a candidate to play Bond in For Your Eyes Only before Roger Moore came back.

John Glen said the strongest of the Australian contenders for Daylights was Andrew Clarke. Clarke was in his early thirties and had enjoyed roles in a battery of familiar Australian shows like The Sullivans, Sons and Daughters, and Prisoner: Cell Block H. It is said that Clarke got to the final round of candidates for Daylights. He was 6'1 and looked rather like a cross between Tom Selleck and the cricketer Alan Border. John Glen said that Clarke was in pole position at one point for The Living Daylights but grew tired of the auditions and contract negotiations in the end. Clarke said that the Bond people wouldn't accept his terms to play 007 so he walked away. A year later, Clarke played Simon Templar in a 1987 TV film pilot called The Saint in Manhattan. On the evidence of this TV film it's difficult to see how Andrew Clarke would have made a good Bond.

I watched The Saint in Manhattan for this book and Clarke is absolutely atrocious with a terrible English accent. He plays Simon Templar as if he's in a stupid comedy film.

Another Australian candidate was 35 year-old Anthony Hamilton - a dancer, model and actor. He took over the main role in the series Cover Up after the death of the series' lead actor Jon-Erik Hexum and had a small part in Jumpin' Jack Flash with Whoopi Goldberg. He was good looking and blond. Hamilton actually looked a bit like the Diagnosis Murder actor Barry Van Dyke. Hamilton was tested by EON and felt to be a good candidate. It is alleged though that Hamilton's sexuality though may have harmed his chances of playing the part. Sadly, things were obviously different in those days. No one would care today if the Bond actor was gay.

Barbara Broccoli is alleged to have personally courted yet another Australian for the role in the shape of Bryan Brown. Brown was said to have no interest in being tied down to a long term contract though so this made any attempt to audition him pointless. Brown was in his late thirties and best known for the television miniseries The Thorn Birds. Brown had a pretty good time at the end of the eighties, appearing in films like Cocktail and Gorillas in the Mist. I can't really see Bryan Brown as James Bond myself.

The French actor Lambert Wilson (who spoke perfect English) was also a candidate for The Living Daylights. He was in his late twenties and had acted with Sean Connery in the 1982 film Five Days One Summer. Wilson screen tested for The Living Daylights opposite Maryam d'Abo as Tatiana Romanova, re-enacting scenes from From Russia with Love. In his memoir, Cubby Broccoli said he liked Lambert Wilson very much and would have happily hired him but Michael G Wilson wasn't convinced and so Lambert Wilson had to be rejected in the end.

The website Den of Geek said that the late Simon MacCorkindale tested for The Living Daylights - although MacCorkindale himself claimed that he was never really seriously pursued for Bond. MacCorkindale was often touted as a potential Bond around this time. He was 35, English, handsome, and quite suave. His profile was pretty good thanks to appearances in American shows like Falcon Crest and the infamous Manimal - where MacCorkindale played a crime fighter who can turn into any animal he desires! His film roles included Jaws 3 and The Riddle of the Sands. One factor that might have gone against MacCorkindale is that he didn't really feel as if he would have been a huge departure from Roger Moore in terms of his looks and that general upper-crust English gentleman adventurer style they both shared. MacCorkindale was one of those actors too who basically gave the same performance in anything he was in. Whether he could have brought anything new to 007 is open to question.

Stephen Hartley had a meeting with EON concerning the part of Bond in 1986. He was only 26 at the time. He would later become best known for playing Supt. Tom Chandler in the police series The Bill. He was tall and dark-haired but looked a bit too sinister to be Bond. Hartley's age probably made him an unrealistic candidate at the time anyway. There is no evidence that he was ever considered again post Daylights. Another potential candidate was Biggles: Adventures in Time star Neil Dickson though it's hard to see how the diminutive Dickson would have got past Cubby's obsessive height stipulations! Dickson was in his mid thirties. Around this time he was about to begin a stint in the US soap opera Dynasty.

The search for Bond in The Living Daylights became so labyrinthe in the end that even American soap stars like John James and Michael Nader were said to be under consideration. Literally half cast of Dynasty was rumoured to be in contention to play Bond! Dirk Benedict, one of the stars of the popular action TV show The A-team, claims that he turned down the chance to replace Roger Moore as Bond in the eighties but this seems hard to believe. Benedict was in his early forties around this time. Benedict did work in London when he made a 1984 episode of the TV show Hammer House of Mystery and Suspense (known in the United States as Fox Mystery Theater) so it is possible I suppose that Benedict had some contact with the Bond people while he was in Blighty.

The silly season in the British tabloids concerning the search for Bond naturally threw up some bizarre stories and suggestions that had no basis in fact. One of the tabloids declared that television smoothie Peter Bowles was up for the part but in reality Bowles was far too old to be a viable candidate. An even more outlandish story had cricket superstar Ian Botham gunning for the part of 007. The chances of Ian Botham playing Bond were absolutely zero!

At some point during the casting process, Timothy Dalton became available again when his theatrical schedule unexpectedly cleared. Cubby Broccoli, who was clearly not convinced by any of the other candidates, decided to approach Dalton again and offer him the part of Bond in The Living Daylights. Cubby offered to push the production of The Living Daylights back by nearly two months so that Timothy could fufil his obligation to appear in the film Brenda Starr. This was now the FOURTH time that EON had spoken to Dalton about becoming Bond - stretching right back to the late 1960s. Surprisingly though, Dalton was still not completely convinced he should take the role. Time was running out at this point so Broccoli continued to test actors - some it seems as a deliberate ploy to persuade Dalton to make a decision.

Robert Bathurst, later best known for the television show Cold Feet, said he tested to play Bond for The Living Daylights but thought it was only to put pressure on Timothy Dalton to make a decision. Bathurst was about 30 at the time and had mostly appeared in comedy shows. "Oh, that was such a ludicrous audition," said Bathurst. "I could never have done it - Bond actors are always very different to me. But some casting director persuaded me to go. The thing was, they already had Timothy Dalton. But I think he hadn't signed yet so they wanted to tell him, 'They're still seeing people, you know,' to put pressure on him to sign. I was just an arm-twisting exercise.

Cubby Broccoli's persistence finally paid off and Timothy Dalton signed on to become the fourth official James Bond actor. Dalton later said he was at an airport when he decided to accept the Bond offer. Interestingly, EON insisted that Timothy Dalton do a screen test before he could be officially signed as Bond. Dalton was reluctant to do this and felt that his body of work was more than sufficient evidence for them to judge him. "Look, nobody doubts your talents," Michael G Wilson told Dalton, "but we have to see you as Bond, just to get an idea of what we're dealing with, what we have on camera." Dalton eventually agreed to the test and it all went fine. He scrubbed as well as you might expect and looked preposterously handsome in his test. EON felt like they had made the right choice and were confident that Timothy Dalton was going to be a terrific Bond.

Dalton was at 6'2 the tallest actor to be cast in the part. After the tongue-in-cheek nature of the Roger Moore era, the casting of Dalton was a bold decision by Cubby Broccoli. It automatically guaranteed that the next film would be a less flippant and jovial affair than Roger's movies had been. But would audiences miss the fun and humour? Only time would tell. "I couldn't see myself taking over and not doing it my own way," said Dalton, "to try and capture Fleming's Bond. He's tarnished. He's not a superclean hero. He's not a white knight. He drinks, smokes. He suffers from this thing called accidie, a moral malaise or confusion which makes him... thoroughly like us."

There was no official press conference to unveil Timothy Dalton as Bond. This was a contrast to Pierce Brosnan in 1994 and Daniel Craig in 2005. These days you simply can't imagine them casting a new James Bond actor without arranging a fancy press conference to unveil him. Bond fans (and the media) would feel cheated if this didn't happen. Dalton simply went straight into shooting the film. The press only got to meet Timothy Dalton when a press conference was held during the Daylights shoot in Vienna on October the 5th 1986. Timothy

Dalton and his co-star Maryam d'Abo also posed for photographers with an Aston Martin V8 Volante. Dalton wore a light blue suit (which doesn't feature in the film) and looked fantastic.

Timothy Dalton impressed everyone during the Daylights shoot with his complete lack of ego. He was unfailingly polite and down to earth and there was no diva behaviour at all. More than anything it was Dalton's intensity that impressed the crew after years of jovial Roger Moore extravaganzas. He was game to do many dangerous stunts and threw himself into the action. Daylights received a fairly positive reception from critics with most of them feeling that Timothy Dalton was a welcome change of gear after thirteen years of Roger Moore. Dalton was praised by many critics for bringing the series back to earth and providing a more straight-laced interpretation of the character. Most people seemed to think that Daylights was an excellent film.

The Living Daylights grossed about $190 million worldwide. It was up against the teen vampire horror comedy The Lost Boys at the US box-office but had an $11 million weekend to claim the top spot. In the end, Daylights comfortably outgrossed the previous three Roger Moore films so EON and Cubby Broccoli could be happy that their new era seemed to have made a more than solid start. Dalton's Byronic good looks and moody charm in The Living Daylights briefly seemed set to position him as the definitive screen James Bond. At a fit and athletic 41 years of age, Dalton seemed set to take James Bond well into the 1990s.

THE BACKGROUND RUMBLINGS OF THE TIMOTHY DALTON ERA

Although the script for The Living Daylights had been approached in a somewhat generic way because it was uncertain who would play Bond (and for a time also assumed that Pierce Brosnan would play Bond), the story for the next film was developed in a way to tailor it to Timothy Dalton's presumed strengths. Both Dalton and the writers wanted the next film to be tougher and a bit more harder edged than The Living Daylights. The original title of Timothy Dalton's second Bond film was License Revoked. A poster bearing this title appeared at the Cannes Film Festival. On the first day of shooting, Cubby Broccoli was pictured holding a slate which clearly says License Revoked. However, when market research suggested that the general public didn't know what the word 'revoked' meant this title was dropped in favour of Licence To Kill (a title which obviously adopted the British spelling).

The script for Licence To Kill borrowed a few elements from the Fleming short story The Hildebrand Rarity. The Hildebrand Rarity appeared in the 1960 short story collection For Your Eyes Only. In the story, while on holiday in the Seychelles, Bond falls in with dubious millionaire Milton Krest and is persuaded to join a search for a rare spiked fish known as The Hildebrand Rarity which Krest must find as part of a tax dodge. Krest beats his wife with a whip (Franz Sanchez has a similar habit in Licence To Kill) and poisons countless fish looking for The Hildebrand Rarity and the millionaire will be lucky to survive the boat trip without getting his comeuppance.

It was decided to give the next film a more tropical setting and Michael G. Wilson, initially working with Richard Maibaum but then working alone after a writer's strike, came up with a story that was inspired by Akira Kurosawa's Yojimbo (which in turn inspired films like A Fistful of Dollars). The idea was that Bond would play the villains off against one another to extract revenge for an attack on Felix Leiter. Wilson felt that 'revenge mission' story would be a good mesh for Timothy Dalton's darker take on James Bond. For tax reasons, Licence To kill was made in Mexico and this turned out to be something of an ordeal. There were logistical troubles and Timothy Dalton said he got rather homesick. Because the air was so thin where they were based Cubby Broccoli got ill and had to leave the production. Sadly, this would be Cubby's last involvement with a Bond production.

John Glen and EON were greatly dismayed when Licence To Kill received a 15 certificate in Britain. Four different versions of the film were released with Britain and Europe getting the most watered down version (in that cuts were made to violent scenes). The death of Krest in the decompression chamber (where his head explodes!) was one scene that had to be trimmed. It must have been a slightly new experience for EON to grapple with censors in this fashion. The 15 certificate in Britain was a big blow because James Bond films had always traditionally been enjoyed by children.

Studio cost cutting also (much to the irritation of Cubby Broccoli) threatened to damage Licence To Kill before it had even been released. Robert Peak designed fantastic teaser illustration and art for Licence To Kill but it was all dumped for a cheaper and far less effective campaign. MGM also discarded a campaign created by advertising executive Don Smolen, who had worked in the publicity campaign for eight previous Bond films. Certainly, the North American poster for Licence To Kill that did emerge must rank as one of the worst posters ever produced for Bond and gives you little clue that it's even promoting a James Bond film!

Licence to Kill premiered at the Odeon Leicester Square in London on the 13th of June 1989. Bond fans tend to be divided on Licence To Kill to this day and that was certainly the case with critics in 1989. Sadly, Licence To Kill struggled in the North American blockbuster box-office summer of 1989 (Batman, Indiana Jones and the Last Crusade, Lethal Weapon 2, Ghostbusters 2, Honey I Shrunk the Kids, Star Trek V etc) and was considered to be a financial disappointment there. It made around $34 million in the United States - which was definitely disappointing because Daylights had made over $50 million in America and a number of films made over $100 million at the North American box-office in the amazing movie summer of 1989. It is said that MGM basically withdrew the marketing for Licence To Kill after a week and one can believe that because the picture plainly struggled to hold its position. The eighties Bond films had increasingly static budgets because they were still paying off the interest on Moonraker going over budget. John Glen complained that the static budgets of the Bond films at this time made it difficult to stage all the action in Licence To Kill.

It was definitely an unusual sort of year in 1989 because even films that were not obvious blockbusters like Parenthood and When Harry Met Sally outgrossed Licence To Kill three or four times over in the United States that summer. Licence To Kill's tepid performance in North America was especially galling (and perhaps confusing) for EON because the tougher tone and increased violence was tailored for the American market (where action movies seemed to be becoming more violent all the time). One of the most frustrating things about Licence To Kill's disappointing box-office in North America is that the movie scored high marks with preview audiences in the United States. With a more committed marketing campaign it could (and probably should) have been a much bigger hit.

Amazingly, speculation about Timothy Dalton's future as James Bond began before the dust had even settled on Licence To Kill. The British tabloids ran stories in the summer of 1989 that the studio wanted to replace Dalton with Pierce Brosnan. The shadow of Brosnan increasingly loomed over Timothy Dalton's Bond so heavily that in 1990 a number of people noted that a (soon to be discontinued) cover on John Gardner's latest Bond novel Brokenclaw seemed to illustrate James Bond to look like Pierce Brosnan!

Brosnan's career was stuttering somewhat circa 1989. The films he had made (Nomads, Taffin, The Deceivers) received poor reviews and he was still struggling to escape from the world of TV miniseries. The one bright spot for Brosnan had been the decent 1987 thriller The Fourth Protocol - in which he did well as a ruthless Russian agent on a secret mission to set off a nuclear device in the West. All in all though, Brosnan would probably have bitten your hand off if you'd offered him James Bond in 1989.

After his initial outbursts at NBC, Pierce Brosnan had shown his class by mostly staying silent about losing out on The Living Daylights. He did this largely out of respect for Timothy Dalton - who he personally knew and also liked. Brosnan did though shoot a 007 inspired Diet Coke commercial in 1988 in which he played a James Bondish Milk Tray Man style character who dodges ninjas and hangs on the side of the train before settling down in a carriage to enjoy a can of coke with a beautiful woman.

The speculation about Dalton's future was obviously a consequence of Licence To Kill not doing nearly as well in the United States as the studio and EON might have hoped. While there might conceivably have been a few MGM executives in 1989 who would have been perfectly happy to put Dalton in the ejector seat and hire Pierce Brosnan, there was zero chance of this actually happening. Dalton was under contract to make a third film and still had the full support of Cubby Broccoli and EON.

It is certainly interesting that, despite the mixed reception to Licence To Kill and disappointing North American gross, Cubby Broccoli was intent on a business as usual approach and had no desire for a hiatus or time to stew on the direction the franchise might go. He was also clearly still 100% behind Timothy Dalton. While all these plans were slowly stirred and simmered though, a storm cloud entered the horizon. MGM/UA was sold to Pathé Communications. Danjaq, the Swiss based parent company of EON, sued MGM/UA and its new chairman to protect the TV distribution rights of the James Bond series from being devalued. These legal wrangles would, unknown to anyone at the time, drag on for much longer than expected and have profound consequences for Bond 17. It basically meant that the next Bond film could not be made until these matters were resolved.

In 1992, the newspapers were full of unlikely stories that the Hollywood producer Joel Silver was planning to buy the James Bond franchise and replace Timothy Dalton with Mel Gibson. In the midst of the litigation wrangles it was reported that Cubby Broccoli put his Bond rights up for sale and Silver was one of the interested parties. However, this sale obviously did not go ahead. Broccoli either never planned to sell in the first place, withdrew his offer, or was simply using the threat of a sale as a tactic in his battle with former MGM/UA owner Kirk Kerkorian and MGM's Giancarlo Parretti - an Italian financier who purchased MGM for $1.2 billion in 1990. Parretti was accused of looting the legendary studio, defaulting on the loan payments to Credit Lyonnais, and bringing the studio to near bankruptcy. Less than a year later, Parretti was forced to resign as Chairman and CEO of MGM.

There was more strange speculation around this time when it was reported in the media that a James Bond television show was in the works and that Robert Powell and Lewis Collins were among the actors who had been approached to play James Bond in this proposed show. To the surprise of absolutely no one, these stories turned out to have no basis in fact. Even so, EON took the step of publishing a statement (more of a warning really) in Variety reminding any 'interested parties' that only they (EON) had the legal rights to make films or television shows based on James Bond.

Several years later, during the press junket for the film Tomorrow Never Dies, Pierce Brosnan confessed that in the early 1990s he and a producer friend had approached Kevin McClory with a view to Brosnan playing 007 in a new remake of Thunderball. Nothing came of this because the legal complications were still immense and headache inducing but it did indicate how desperate Pierce Brosnan was to play James Bond. Losing out on The Living Daylights was still something that rankled him. He must have felt like his career would not be complete or even have a proper second act unless he played James Bond. This was certainly a contrast to the men who came before and after him in the 007 franchise. One has the impression that if Timothy Dalton or Daniel Craig had lost out on Bond it honestly wouldn't have bothered them that much. This definitely wasn't the case with Brosnan.

Behind the scenes, in the middle of the litigation quagmire, Cubby Broccoli asked Timothy Dalton what his thoughts were regarding Bond 17. Dalton told Broccoli that he honestly couldn't see himself returning. "Because of the lawsuit, I was free of the contract," said Dalton. "And Mr Broccoli, who I really respected as a producer and as a friend, asked me what I was going to do when it was resolved. I said, 'Look, in all honesty, I don't think that I will continue.' He asked me for my support during that time, which of course, I gave him."

This decision was not set in stone though and Dalton later indicated to Broccoli that he WOULD be interested in returning. This change of heart was in danger of becoming irrelevant though thanks to changes behind the scenes at MGM. John Calley (who was appointed president by the new chairman Frank Mancuso) would eventually take over at MGM and was described as more 'Bond friendly' (in that he was much easier to work with and wanted the cameras rolling on Bond 17 as fast as possible) than his infamous predecessor. The litigation dispute was finally resolved in December 1992. John Calley was eager to get Bond 17 into production. However, Calley was most definitely not eager to see Timothy Dalton back as Bond.

It was reported in the press that John Calley had suggested four names to EON who MGM would find acceptable as James Bond in Bond 17. These names were alleged to be Hugh Grant, Ralph Fiennes, Liam Neeson, and Pierce Brosnan. EON however dug their heels in and insisted that it was up to Timothy Dalton if he wanted to come back. They did not want to be disloyal to Dalton and replace him with another actor. Besides, they thought Dalton was an excellent Bond and deserved a chance to cement his legacy with a third film.

After an appearance in the 1993 film Naked in New York, Timothy Dalton made a TV movie called Red Eagle (aka Lie Down with Lions). Red Eagle (which also featured Jürgen Prochnow and Omar Sharif) was a spy drama based on a book by Ken Follett. Dalton then signed to play Rhett Butler in Scarlett - a TV miniseries sequel to Gone with the Wind. The cast of Scarlett included Sean Bean. Unknown to anyone at the time, Bean was soon to become one of the actors vying to replace Dalton as 007. While on the set of Scarlett, Timothy Dalton read the Michael France Bond 17 draft called Goldeneye. Dalton enjoyed the script and thought it would make a good film. He knew that he needed to make a decision regarding his participation in Bond 17. Things were moving fast and they needed to know if he was in or out.

Timothy Dalton now made the decision not to return as James Bond. Many years later he said that his decision was prompted by the fact that he only wanted to come back and make one more film whereas EON didn't see the point of this. "Cubby Broccoli asked if I would come back," said Dalton, "and I said, 'Well, I've actually changed my mind a little bit. I think that I'd love to do one. Try and take the best of the two that I have done, and consolidate them into a third.' And he said, quite rightly, 'Look, Tim. You can't do one. There's no way, after a five-year gap between movies that you can come back and just do one. You'd have to plan on four or five.' And I thought, oh, no, that would be the rest of my life. Too much. Too long. So I respectfully declined."

In April 1994, Timothy Dalton released a statement confirming the end of his tenure as Bond. 'Even though the producers have always made it clear to me that they want me to resume my role in their next James Bond feature, I have now made this difficult decision. As an actor, I believe it is now time to leave that wonderful image behind and accept the challenge of new ones. The Broccolis have been good to me as producers. They have been more special as friends.' EON released their own statement in which they said - 'We have never thought of anyone but Timothy as the star of the 17th

James Bond film. We understand his reasons and we will honor his decision.'

The early drafts of the film that became Goldeneye had been written for Timothy Dalton. This had all changed now. Goldeneye would now mark the debut of a new Bond actor. But who would that actor be? A familiar face - just as he had been with Daylights - was a formidable favourite.

GOLDENEYE

The search for Timothy Dalton's replacement quickly began but it was not to prove the most complex or lengthy task EON had ever faced when it came to finding a new James Bond actor. Martin Campbell, who had been hired to direct Goldeneye, said it was always pretty obvious to them that Pierce Brosnan was going to do it so the other interviews and auditions had a curious feel of going through the motions. "To be honest with Pierce, even though we went around and met people, I'm a bit vague about it because in the back of our heads we knew Pierce was going to play it, there was no-one else," said Campbell.

Pierce Brosnan's only mildly serious rival for Timothy Dalton's tux was said to be Liam Neeson but Neeson wasn't very enthusiastic at all. Neeson said he was heavily 'courted' by the Bond people but ruled himself out of the running. Neeson was about to get married and didn't want to become involved in something as time consuming as making James Bond films. He also had little interest in making action films at the time. Neeson's attitude to appearing in action films would obviously change many years later in the veteran phase of his career. These days Liam Neeson seems to make nothing but action films!

I must confess that I never quite understood why Liam Neeson always seemed to be so high on studio lists when it came to

Bond. Sure, he's a very fine actor but Neeson never personally struck me as very James Bondian. Around the time that Goldeneye was being planned, Neeson had recently featured in acclaimed dramas like Schindler's List and Husbands and Wives so you could probably forgive him if he felt that he didn't need Bond. His career was going more than fine as it was.

Jeremy Northam was contacted about the possibility of playing Bond in Goldeneye. He was dark-haired and handsome and a solid candidate. There's no doubt that he looked the part. Northam was in his early thirties at the time and about to appear in the cyber thriller The Net with Sandra Bullock. Northam later said that he declined to pursue the part of Bond because of a family bereavement. He doesn't appear to have any regrets and has remained a very private sort of actor who doesn't seem to court fame. Jeremy Northam appeared in numerous films (An Ideal Husband, Amistad, Enigma, Gosford Park etc) so declining to pursue Bond didn't have any negative effect on his career at all. In 2007 he was in the film The Invasion with Daniel Craig. This is the movie Craig was making when he was cast as Bond.

James Purefoy was another actor on the radar of EON at this time. He was 29 years-old and yet to make his film debut although he was becoming a busy British television actor. Purefoy was handsome and suave and had a good sense of humour. He could potentially have made a very good James Bond. Purefoy tested for Goldeneye but was obviously not chosen to play 007 in the end. At this stage though Purefoy still had time on his side and would be a stronger candidate next time around. Purefoy was definitely someone that EON liked and kept tabs on. It's not that difficult at all to picture Purefoy as Bond.

Adrian Paul was sort of like the nineties version of Lewis Collins (though Lewis Collins was clearly a better and more versatile actor) in that he had a lot of support from the public regarding his 007 aspirations and played a Bondish sort of role on television. Since 1992 he had been the lead in the Highlander television show. He was a martial artist, model, and actor and sort of resembled a young Sean Connery. Paul was in his mid thirties and would have snapped your hand off if you'd offered him the part of James Bond. Though he has suggested he had some contact with the Bond people around the time of Goldeneye it doesn't appear that Adrian Paul ever came tremendously close to the part. The main liability of Adrian Paul was the fact that he wasn't exactly Timothy Dalton in the thesping department.

Colin Wells was a young actor who EON allegedly employed to play Bond in auditions for prospective leading ladies. It is said that Wells was first noticed by EON while performing at Glasgow Citizen`s Theatre and invited to audition for Bond in 1994. He obviously didn't get the part. In the late nineties, Wells was in CI5: The New Professionals - a forgotten sequel to the old Lewis Collins/Martin Shaw show. A few years later Wells was a regular in television shows like Hollyoaks and Crossroads. He never really became much of a star. Though quite handsome, Colin Wells seemed to lack a certain something for Bond. He seemed a little bit too ordinary.

Ralph Fiennes, then in his early thirties and already establishing himself as a major film star, said he had an informal chat with Cubby Broccoli about playing Bond in Goldeneye. "There was a conversation that was great and a meeting with Cubby Broccoli, that was terrific. I think that's all I can say, except that it didn't lead to anything on both sides. I don't think I felt ready to commit and I think they were looking at Pierce [Brosnan]." Fiennes didn't really feel like he was right for Bond and hardly needed the work anyway as he was much in demand. He probably would have been crazy to constrict himself to making Bond films at the time. Years later he played M in the last Daniel Craig films.

Nathaniel Parker had some contact with EON concerning the part of Bond for Goldeneye. At the time he was about 32 and had appeared in films like The Bodyguard and Hamlet. Parker had black hair and was very handsome. He certainly looked the part. Parker was later best known for his role in The Inspector Lynley Mysteries on television. He has also narrated the Young Bond audiobooks. Parker has remained a very busy and successful actor so losing out on Bond didn't see him plunge into obscurity like others who have been considered for the role in the past. I suspect that Nathaniel Parker might have been a fairly solid Bond but it doesn't seem that he came especially close to securing the role.

Contemporary articles about Goldeneye often state that Paul McGann was the runner-up and would have played the part if Brosnan had not chosen to do it. However, McGann, who is famously honest and open about his career, has never spoken about James Bond and Martin Campbell denied that McGann was auditioned for the part. Still, one would presume that McGann was at least considered or floated on some sort of list (and if we know one thing about James Bond casting sessions by now it's that the list of Bond candidates can be very long). McGann was in his thirties, already a film actor, good looking, and a fine actor to boot. The one thing that might have gone against him was his height (5'9). In 1996 McGann did get to portray an iconic hero when he played the Doctor in a Doctor Who television film.

The former boxer Glenn McCrory said that he read for the part of James Bond in 1994. McCrory was about 30 at the time. He was the IBF cruiserweight world champion in 1989 and in one of his last fights fought the great Lennox Lewis. McCrory had launched an acting career after his boxing career finished and his credits included Our Friends in the North (which featured Daniel Craig) and Gerry Anderson's Space Precinct. McCrory said that one of the EON casting people was amused by his Geordie accent and he reminded her that the first Bond had been Scottish! McCrory was very tall and a good looking chap but you'd imagine him playing Bond was always a bit of a long shot to say the least. McCrory's acting career took a back seat in the end when he got a well paid boxing commentary gig on Sky television.

Mark Frankel was another young British actor who was considered for Goldeneye. He was in his early thirties and probably best known for the film Leon the Pig Farmer. Frankel played a very James Bondish character in the daft 1994 action TV show Fortune Hunter. Mark Frankel was an incredibly handsome man and certainly looked like James Bond but whether he had the acting chops to make an interesting 007 is open to question. He was definitely someone on the EON radar though and an obvious candidate purely for his looks alone. Sadly, Mark Frankel tragically died in a motorcycle accident in London in 1996. He was just 34 years-old.

It is often alleged by Bond fans that Barbara Broccoli wanted to cast Sean Bean as James Bond in Goldeneye. Cubby was in poor health by this time and didn't have long to live and so Barbara was essentially picking up her father's baton when it came to the franchise from this point in. However, Barbara didn't yet have the final say on casting (as she later would the next time the part of 007 came up). The story that Barbara wanted Sean Bean is of course impossible to verify. The explanation for this theory is presumably that Sean Bean was somewhat like Barbara's beloved Daniel Craig - blond and a slightly left-field Bond candidate! Sean Bean said he didn't audition for Bond but he did imply in a Goldeneye special hosted by Jonathan Ross that he got close to the part. Bean was about 35 at the time and best known for the television period adventure show Sharpe. He was obviously in the mix for 007 but, as we know, ended up playing 006 in the movie.

It is occasionally still reported that Alan Rickman tested to become Bond in Goldeneye. This is not correct. Rickman was offered the part of Alec Trevelyan but turned it down because he feared becoming too typecast as villains. It's not as if he needed the work anyway. In the early drafts of Goldeneye the character of Alec Trevelyan was older and more of a mentor to Bond. Anthony Hopkins turned the part down originally and then Rickman obviously did too. It seems that the drafts made Alec Trevelyan younger and younger in the end. Sean Bean, who finally played the part, was actually six years younger than Goldeneye's Bond actor Pierce Brosnan. It's a slight shame really that Rickman didn't do Goldeneye because Alan Rickman playing a Bond villain would have been fantastic.

There was a lot of speculation in the media about Hugh Grant becoming the new Bond around this time. Grant was about 34 and had already been in several films. He became a big star with the success of Four Weddings and a Funeral in 1994. Grant has said though that he was never offered the part or approached about the role. EON evidently didn't think Grant was macho enough to be Bond and you probably can't blame them for that view. Grant was pretty typecast as a romcom comedic actor for a time but has showed some impressive acting chops in later roles. It's hard to imagine Hugh Grant as James Bond to be honest. He didn't really feel like a completely natural fit for the part.

Charles Dance claims that he was asked to test for Bond when Timothy Dalton departed. He said his agent told him to decline the invitation and so this is what he did. "She (my agent) might have been right." said Dance. "I don't know that it would have ruined my career, but I am not sure I was right (for the part) anyway." Dance was in his late forties around the time that Goldeneye was in development so appears to be a pretty bizarre candidate. Maybe EON had him in mind to play Alec Trevelyan rather than Bond. Dance had already been in a Bond film thanks to his small role in For Your Eyes Only.

Jason Isaacs was one of the many British actors vaguely considered for Goldeneye. He was in his early thirties and still primarily a television actor at the time. In 1992 he starred in the BBC drama Civvies with Peter O'Toole and appeared in many TV shows around this time like Boon and Inspector Morse. Isaacs doesn't appear to have got especially close to winning the part although in later years he was someone that cropped up a lot on Bond forums when fans suggested actors they thought would make a good 007. Jason Isaacs has enjoyed a busy and successful career as an actor on stage and screen so losing out on James Bond wasn't something that had any negative effect on his career at all. Trivia - Isaacs is good friends with Daniel Craig and once played his lover in a play for a year.

Greg Wise had a meeting with the Bond producers in 1994 to discuss the part of 007. He was 28 at the time and still a television actor but on the cusp of making the jump to films with two period romps (the most notable of which was Sense and Sensibility). "When I was 28 and I was doing a film where I had a big moustache, I met the producers for Bond," said Wise. "And about two weeks later – these are the days of faxes – I got a fax from a journalist at the Sunday Times saying 'Mr Wise, I understand you're training with the special forces for your upcoming role as James Bond'." As a consequence of this speculation Greg Wise had very short odds for a time with bookmakers but he didn't get the part in the end - nor did he become a candidate again in the future despite expressing a desire for another chance. Wise blamed his period sideburns for ruining his 007 dream when he met the producers.

Despite all the interviews and casting calls, a familiar name was always the red hot favourite to take the 007 mantle from Timothy Dalton. Goldeneye was definitely the easiest Bond casting call to predict. Step forward Pierce Brosnan - still only 41 years-old and (here was the REALLY crucial part) acceptable to both EON and MGM. Brosnan didn't even have to audition for the part because EON obviously still had his 1986 screen test in the vault. There was something inevitable about Pierce Brosnan becoming James Bond. It was just something that always seemed destined to happen one day. In May 1994, Brosnan dodged media questions linking him to the part of Bond but this was simply misdirection before an official announcement. Brosnan already knew he had the part in the bag.

In the summer of 1994, in one of the worst kept secrets in the world, Pierce Brosnan was officially announced as the new James Bond. The night before the press conference to announce the new James Bond, Brosnan had been photographed by the media dining in a London restaurant. You probably didn't have to be Hercule Poirot to deduce that Brosnan was in town for the Bond press conference. Brosnan had finally won the part he seemed destined to play from the moment he met Cubby Broccoli on the set of For Your Eyes Only all those years ago. The Bond series had come full circle. Dalton replaced Brosnan and now Brosnan was replacing Dalton.

Believe it or not, there was actually a lot of scepticism regarding Goldeneye before it was released. When the cast was unveiled, the British press noted the absence of big stars and even suspected that this film was maybe being made on the cheap or something. Nothing could have been further from the actual truth. Goldeneye had a budget of $60 million and was fully committed to reviving the fortunes of the mothballed Bond franchise. Far from hammering the final nail into 007's coffin, Goldeneye sparked a revival in the franchise and made James Bond feel bigger than it had been since the halycon days of Roger Moore battling Jaws in The Spy Who Loved Me and Moonraker.

Goldeneye had two excellent Bond Girls in Famke Janssen and Isabelle Scorupco, a terrific bungee jump opening, a fantastic tank chase, an amazing title sequence by Daniel Kleinman, model work by the great Derek Meddings, a grand scale climax shot at the Arecibo Observatory in Puerto Rico, and plenty of Bondian trappings. Goldeneye also reflected changing times with a female M and reflections on whether Bond might be a dinosaur of the Cold War. Pierce Brosnan proved to be a safe pair of hands as the new James Bond. He was lighter than Timothy Dalton but not as flippant as Roger Moore. Brosnan was somewhere in the middle and proved to be the right man for the franchise at this potentially tricky juncture.

In 1996, the maverick Irish film producer Kevin McClory declared in Variety magazine that he had plans to make a renegade Bond film to go up against Pierce Brosnan's second

007 film. "I'm back in the Bond business because I have a couple of films I want to direct and Bond can provide the finance," said McClory. "I didn't want to make another Bond film, but now that I've come this far, I'm enjoying it immensely. The film will be called Warhead 2000 and an actor has been chosen to play Bond. But we won't announce it yet to keep the competition in the dark. No, it's not Sean Connery. He's too old for the part now. But he has said he would play the villain in a James Bond film if the price was right." As ever with Kevin McClory though, there was a huge gulf between his public pronouncements and cold hard reality.

The remarkable thing about McClory's plan to make a rival James Bond film in the 1990s is that he was backed by SONY - who were now headed by a certain John Calley! "We are satisfied that McClory has the right to make James Bond," said Calley. MGM were understandably furious that Calley, who obviously had insider knowledge on the Bond films having worked for MGM, was now apparently plotting against the official Bond franchise. Roland Emmerich and Dean Devlin, the team behind Independence Day and Godzilla, were supposedly working on the new renegade James Bond film according to media reports.

McClory's new Bond film was alleged to involve a plot in which Blofeld hijacks ships in the Bermuda Triangle to steal nuclear weapons. The media widely reported that Liam Neeson and Timothy Dalton were vying to play James Bond in the movie and that Sean Connery was in talks to play the villain. It's safe to say that none of this was verifiable and about as likely to happen as Ian Botham being cast as Bond in The Living Daylights. Kevin McClory, who was amusingly called the "Rip Van Winkle of copyright laws" by MGM in the court case, eventually lost his legal battle to make another Bond film and SONY eventually threw the towel in. The legal wrangles had a nice bonus for EON as they ended up with the rights to Casino Royale (the one Fleming novel that had eluded them).

Kevin McClory had mentioned Timothy Dalton as someone he

was interested in when it came to James Bond candidates for his Warhead film. The chances of this happening were remote. Not only had Timothy Dalton moved on from Bond but he was also friends with the Broccoli family. There is no way Dalton would have been disloyal to EON and the Broccolis by appearing in a rival James Bond film. The strange headlines concerning Warhead in the late 1990s were a reminder that no one can ever completely escape from the shadow of James Bond once they have played the part. This was certainly the case with Timothy Dalton and all the dubious headlines linking him to Kevin McClory.

In the unlikely event that Warhead 2000 had gone ahead it seems highly doubtful that the other alleged candidate Liam Neeson would have taken the role. If he declined to be considered for Goldeneye why would he want to do a renegade Bond film? Neeson was also friends with Pierce Brosnan and probably wouldn't have had much enthusiasm for a 'Battle of the Bonds' with his pal. It doesn't seem outlandish to think that Sean Connery could have played Bond in Warhead 2000 and there were certainly plenty of media stories at the time which suggested that Connery could be enticed back. He was in his late sixties but still looked terrific (not to mention spry) in movies like Entrapment and The Rock at the time. Look at Harrison Ford. He's pushing eighty and yet still playing Indiana Jones!

Believe it or not a couple of other names were linked to the part of Bond in Warhead 2000 but both of these seemed as unlikely as any prospects of the actual film going into production. Christian Burgess was a little known British actor who was vaguely connected to playing 007 for McClory in the media. As far I can tell, what seems to have touted Burgess as a potential Bond is the fact that he played an ex-SAS action man in a forgotten 1989 show called Saracen. He was also in one of those MacGyver television movies.

Christian Burgess was actually in the long running BBC children's show Grange Hill by the late nineties. Grange Hill to

Bond! That would have been an unlikely journey. Burgess was dark haired and quite attractive but you wouldn't say that he screamed James Bond. He looked a bit like that late eighties Simon Templar actor Simon Dutton. By the way, just in case you are wondering, I can't find any evidence that Simon Dutton was ever considered for Bond!

The other actor allegedly in contention for Warhead 2000 was Sean's son Jason Connery. Jason Connery was in his thirties and best known for replacing Michael Praed in the eighties TV show Robin of Sherwood. In 1990, Jason Connery played Ian Fleming in a daft TV movie called Spymaker: The Secret Life of Ian Fleming. The career of Jason Connery never really seemed to catch light and by the latter half of the 1990s he was making appearances in British TV shows like Casualty. It's dreadfully unfair to make any comparisons but Jason Connery never had his father's acting chops or machismo. In the unlikely event of Warhead 2000 going before the cameras you'd have to think that they could have found any number of actors who would have been better qualified than Jason Connery.

CASINO ROYALE

When he become Bond, Pierce Brosnan signed a three film contract with an option for a fourth. In comparison to the Roger Moore era (and even the brief Tim Dalton era) there wasn't much background noise when it came to next Bond rumours during the Brosnan years. There was never any thought of replacing Brosnan at all during his first three pictures because they all did well at the box-office and Brosnan was a popular and well regarded 007. At the time Brosnan was pretty much lauded as the man who saved the franchise.

A section of Bond fans would later (after Brosnan no longer had the role) attempt to rewrite history and suggest that

Brosnan was a terrible and laughable Bond but this is patently nonsense. Most people felt that Brosnan was by far the best thing about films like The World Is Not Enough and Die Another Day. It wasn't Brosnan's fault that he didn't have better scripts or directors on those pictures. Brosnan bashing is largely a retrospective construct because his press and notices were mostly excellent when he was Bond. A strange phenomenon with James Bond actors is that their Bond performances seem to be more harshly judged once they no longer have the role and are consigned to history! Brosnan was sort of like a composite of previous Bonds and while it's perfectly fair for some fans to see this as a weakness rather a strength it is plainly ridiculous to say that Brosnan was some sort of bizarre interlude a protesting world had to endure for seven years.

After he completed shooting The World Is Not Enough, Brosnan's contract was slightly up in the air but he seemed fairly certain to do the next film. There is evidence though that EON did look at other options lest they should need a new Bond. There was a lot of speculation about Jonathan Cake coming under consideration in the late nineties as a possible replacement for Brosnan. Cake was in his early thirties and had just earned praise for his performance as Oswald Mosley (Sir Oswald Ernald Mosley, 6th Baronet of Ancoats, was a British politician who rose to fame in the 1920s as a Member of Parliament and later in the 1930s became leader of the British Union of Fascists) in a 1998 Channel 4 miniseries. Cake was dark-haired and sort of dashing (in an anachronistic way) but he later denied that he had tested for Bond.

Another actor alleged to have been contacted in the late nineties was Linus Roache. He was about 35 at the time and best known for the 1994 film Priest. Roache later appeared in a number of Hollywood films. One of his most famous roles was as Thomas Wayne in Christopher Nolan's Batman Begins. Someone who was definitely contacted by EON concerning Bond was Dougray Scott. Scott was about 35 at the time and had just appeared in the films Gregory's Two Girls and Deep

Impact. In a 2006 interview, Scott said - "They first talked to me about it five years ago but then Pierce Brosnan wanted another go." This would suggest that Scott was spoken to about Bond in 2001 and might well have got the part if Brosnan hadn't come back. Scott was desperately unlucky when he was cast as Wolverine in The X-Men but had to pull out when Mission Impossible 2 (in which Scott played the villain) went over schedule. An unknown Australian actor named Hugh Jackman replaced Dougray Scott as Wolverine and the rest is history.

John Barrowman said he auditioned for James Bond in 2002. Barrowman, who was born in Glasgow but brought up in the United States, was in his early thirties and known for musical theatre and the soap opera Central Park West at the time. "I actually met with the Broccoli family," said Barrowman. "I did the audition in my Scottish accent, to emulate Sean Connery. They were bowled over, but said I'd have to wait years to be right for the part." Barrowman's most famous role came three years later when he played Captain Jack Harkness in Doctor Who. Another Scottish actor who had a meeting about Bond around this time was Gerard Butler. Butler was in his early thirties at the time. One of his first film roles was a small part as a sailor in Tomorrow Never Dies. Butler later made a lot of action films but never became a serious Bond candidate.

There was a lot of talk in the media of Russell Crowe, now world famous thanks to his role as Maximus Decimus Meridius in Ridley Scott's film Gladiator, becoming the next Bond but this was obviously just paper talk. Crowe was probably too famous to be a Bond candidate and hardly needed the work anyway. The British tabloids are never shy of armchair Bond casting and in 2002 ventured that pop star turned soap actor Martin Kemp was being lined up to replace Brosnan. This silly story had no basis in fact. Equally spurious were reports that a young British actor named Jason Durr was in pole position to replace Brosnan. Durr was 34 and played PC/DC Mike Bradley in the Yorkshire-based police drama series Heartbeat. The Daily Star reported that Durr had auditioned for Bond and planned to quit Heartbeat to pursue his Bond dream. It's hard to imagine that Jason Durr was ever really in serious contention to be James Bond.

Other names floated in the media concerning the Bond gig included Jude Law. Law was quick to distance himself from such claims and said he didn't feel he was right for Bond. Jude Law had a flourishing A'list film career so there was zero chance of him signing up to make Bond films instead. A few years later Law turned down a chance to be Superman for similar sort of reasons. Showbiz Ireland reported in 2003 that the young Irish actor Jonathan Rhys-Meyers (then becoming quite well known after Velvet Goldmine and Bend it Like Beckham) had auditioned for Bond and was most likely going to replace Brosnan. Alarm bells rang for Bond fans though when Showbiz Ireland couldn't even get Barbara Broccoli's name right. The report felt spurious to say the least. Years later Rhys-Meyers said he wouldn't like to play Bond but he would like to be a Bond villain.

Media reports also suggested that the English actor Nick Moran was in contention to be the next Bond. Moran was in his thirties and had come to prominence through his role as Eddie the card shark in Lock, Stock and Two Smoking Barrels. It seems highly doubtful indeed though that Nick Moran was ever a James Bond candidate. Colin Salmon made a determined pitch to become the next Bond around this time. Salmon portrayed Robinson in the Brosnan Bond films and apparently sometimes played Bond in auditions for EON to test actresses. Though he claimed the public were behind him there was never much traction to Salmon's Bond aspirations. He was probably already too old anyway. Salmon would have been about 44 by the time the next film actually came out. Salmon has been a credible action star though in other movies. It would have felt rather weird for Bond fans if Charles Robinson had suddenly become James Bond in the next movie!

Although the Pierce Brosnan era started very well with

Goldeneye, it rather flattered to deceive in the end. Tomorrow Never Dies was very entertaining (with an excellent performance by Brosnan) but strangely forgettable all the same while The World Is Not Enough, the PTS aside, was rather average. As for 2002's Die Another Day, well that is a book in and of itself. Die Another Die quickly became one of the most reviled films (though it actually made a lot of money and got decent reviews) in Bond history with its invisible Aston Martin, CGI parasurfing (which looked like a cut scene from an MSDOS game), Toby Stephens in a Robocop suit, and Madonna fencing cameo. Die Another Day, the 40th anniversary Bond movie, was supposed to be Brosnan's The Spy Who Loved Me but it obviously didn't quite pan out that way. Lewis Gilbert and Cubby Broccoli could have made Die Another Day a fantastic Bond movie but Lee Tamahori and Barbara Broccoli most assuredly could not.

Die Another Day, though profitable, was an especially silly entry in the series and seemed to indicate that a rethink of the franchise was in order. The obvious solution was simply to make a better film next time and allow Brosnan to gracefully bow out of the franchise on better terms. However, Barbara Broccoli didn't have the patience or the desire for this plan. She wanted to take immediate and drastic action. Barbara and Michael G Wilson decided that a reboot of the franchise was the only solution to the creative malaise that had resulted in Die Another Day. They wanted to draw a line under Die Another Day and start all over again. This meant that Brosnan would have to be let go. The decision by EON to put Brosnan in the ejector seat is believed to have been made in 2003. It took a while though for this to become official.

It was all rather rough on Pierce Brosnan - who probably deserved better treatment. Brosnan later complained that he had been fired via a short telephone call from Barbara Broccoli and Wilson. He said he felt like he had been 'kicked to the kerb'. While no one would say that the Brosnan films, in terms of their quality, constituted an especially vintage era for the franchise, the actor had resurrected Bond in 1995 after a long hiatus and was exceptionally popular in the role. It was not really Brosnan's fault that EON didn't hire better writers and directors during his tenure.

Brosnan was also frustrated by the fact that he never seemed to be allowed to exert any creative control of his own on the franchise - which was remarkable given that he became a successful producer himself! The only Bond actor who seems to have exerted a creative control over the franchise is Daniel Craig. Craig practically became a co-producer on his movies and enjoyed considerable input into the scripts, choice of writers, choice of director, and even the artist to do the theme song. Timothy Dalton and Pierce Brosnan could only dream of such influence.

The sour note that ended Brosnan's tenure as Bond was a great shame because it robbed the series of someone who could have been a great ambassador and elder statesman for the franchise in the way that Roger Moore was in his last decades. Barbara Broccoli and Michael G Wilson both had their own reasons for feeling that a reboot of the Bond series was an attractive proposition. Broccoli, for her part, desperately wanted to cast Daniel Craig as Bond while Wilson had always quite liked the idea of doing a film where Bond was a younger agent new to the service. As we have noted already, he had floated this concept in the 1980s after Roger Moore's tenure came to an end but Cubby Broccoli vetoed the suggestion. The fact that EON had finally acquired the rights to Fleming's first Bond novel Casino Royale (previously adapted as a 1954 CBS television film and also as a big-budget headache inducing comedy movie in 1967) gave them a tailor made story to launch a completely new era of Bond.

When the Daniel Craig era began back in 2006 there was a sense that Bond had fallen behind the times because of the Jason Bourne films. The Bourne Identity, a 2002 Doug Liman thriller based on a book by Robert Ludlam, was about an amnesiac spy (played by Matt Damon) who travels through Europe trying to unravel his identity as a number of assassins and the CIA follow his trail. The Bourne Identity showed that you didn't need hundreds of millions of dollars to make a great action thriller. It had fantastic car chases, brutal fight sequences, and a compelling story. The Bourne Identity had a kinetic energy at times that the recent Bond films seemed to lack. 2004's sequel The Bourne Supremacy was also a critical and box-office success. The shaky camera style of new director Paul Greengrass was not universally loved by everyone but there was no question that The Bourne Supremacy was a rollicking ride and a terrific action film. The Bourne films were tough, mean, and lean and Bond, the producers decided, had to follow suit if the franchise was to stay relevant.

The loyalty and devotion of Barbara Broccoli to Daniel Craig could never be overestimated. Daniel Craig was unveiled as Bond in 2005 but the genesis of his casting went way back to 1998. It was in 1998 that Barbara Broccoli first became aware of Daniel Craig when she watched the film Elizabeth. Broccoli was captivated by this stocky fair-haired actor with the face of a boxer. She watched everything Craig had done and decided that he could be Bond one day. Daniel Craig was the only person that Barbara wanted for Casino Royale. However, there were still dozens of other actors who were sounded out, auditioned, and interviewed. In fact, as far as the Bond casting circus goes, Casino Royale become something of a marathon. They talked to literally everyone at some point or other.

There was an awful lot of speculation in the media in 2004 that the Australian actor Eric Bana was going to be the next Bond. Bana was about 37 and had appeared in films like Chopper, Black Hawk Down, and Hulk. Around this time he was actually shooting the Spielberg film Munich - where one of his co-stars was a certain Daniel Craig. Though he appeared to be a plausible 007 candidate on the face of it, Bana quickly distanced himself from the speculation and said he had no interest in the part. Bana seemed rather perplexed and irritated by all the speculation about him becoming Bond and said he had no idea where the stories came from. The alleged source of the rumours apparently came from an announcer at an Australian motor sport event calling Bana the next James Bond. After this flippant comments things rather snowballed.

James Purefoy, a candidate for Goldeneye, was interviewed again for the part of Bond after Brosnan was axed. Purefoy had recently appeared in films like A Knight's Tale and Resident Evil and was still a pretty good Bond candidate. What went against him was his age. He was rather on the old side now for the youngish Bond angle that the producers were vaguely aiming for in the next film. Australian movie website MOVIEHOLE.NET reported in 2005 that Purefoy was the producer's number one choice for the role but this obviously didn't turn out to be the case - unless of course Purefoy rebuffed the interest.

Of his latest (and last) Bond interview, Purefoy said - "The room is very Bondesque: wood panelling, big table. You sit there trying to be as serious and panther-like as you can, just letting them look at you. They asked what I thought should be changed and I was eight minutes into my soliloquy when I noticed they were all staring at my legs. Being a ludicrous, over-excited boy of 42, I was kicking them like a child. I realised there was no hope."

In a 2020 interview with The Independent, James Purefoy said of Bond - "There have been jobs, Bond being one of them, where you get very close to getting something and then you start pulling away because the ramifications of what would happen if you got it become a little troubling. The closer I got to Bond, the more I wasn't really sure. From what I gather, [Daniel Craig] turned it down two or three times because of a similar thing – being uncomfortable with being locked into a massive corporate world where you're gonna spend more time publicising the movie and wearing watches and suits and having to go to photoshoots and publicity drives and you end up having to deal with a lot of stuff that you'd just really rather not deal with because it's not your job. It's not what you do. What you do is exist as somebody else between action and cut. That's the purest and most interesting part of the job. I kind of wish it had never been found out that I'd gone up for Bond. It has plagued my life – the job that I didn't get."

Dougray Scott was considered again by EON when they decided to give Brosnan the boot but the plans to do Casino Royale and depict a younger Bond meant that Scott was slightly too old for the part now and so wasn't a viable candidate anymore. According to the website CommanderBond, David Morrissey was a verified candidate to replace Pierce Brosnan. Morrissey was an excellent actor and had just appeared in Girl with a Pearl Earring and Captain Corelli's Mandolin at the time. At 40 years-old though he was little on the mature side for what EON had in mind for the next film. As his part in The Walking Dead later indicated, Morrissey would probably make a much better Bond villain than 007.

Martin Campbell, who was back to direct Casino Royale, said that they briefly spoke to Ewan McGregor very early on in the casting process. Ewan McGregor was in his thirties and a common suggestion at the time when it came to people who might replace Brosnan. There was never any sense though that McGregor was a serious candidate. He later said that he was not very keen on the idea of being entangled in another franchise after only just finishing the Star Wars prequels. Ewan McGregor didn't need the work anyway. He was a very busy and successful actor. One might venture that, despite his fame and success, Ewan McGregor was a trifle too wooden to be a great Bond.

There was a lot of speculation about Orlando Bloom becoming the next Bond around this time. He was still in his twenties and riding high thanks to his roles in two huge franchises - The Lord of the Rings and Pirates of the Caribbean. Though he has often said he would love to play Bond there is no evidence that Bloom was ever approached or considered. Truth be told, Bloom was already too famous and expensive by 2004/2005 and he simply wasn't what Barbara Broccoli was looking for anyway. She wanted a tougher and grittier Bond and Bloom simply didn't tick those boxes.

If you had to cast a new James Bond around this time there were two very obvious candidates who seemed to stand out from the pack. These two candidates were Clive Owen and Hugh Jackman. So what happened to them? Were they in contention? Clive Owen was nearing 40 at the time that Casino Royale was marinating in development. He had been spoken of as a Bond candidate ever since the 1998 film Croupier - which Owen's character spent most of in a tux working in a casino. Croupier was practically like a feature length Bond audition. There is no doubt that Owen looked the part of Bond and he had further enhanced his Bond credentials by appearing in a series of BMW shorts called The hire in which he played a suave Bondish action man. After appearing in films like The Bourne Identity and Gosford Park, Owen was becoming a leading man and starred in King Arthur and Beyond Borders. In 2004 there were even media rumours that Owen had already been cast as Bond. These rumours were obviously false.

The truth concerning Clive Owen is tricky to discern because he has contradicted himself on the issue. Owen said in an interview with Glamour Magazine that he consistently turned down Bond but in other interviews he has claimed that he was never approached. The general truth seems to be that Clive Owen was never that fussed about Bond and EON were never that fussed about Clive Owen. It could be that EON thought Owen was a little old for what they had in mind for Casino Royale. Maybe they thought he would be too expensive. "It was never on the radar," said Owen. "There was nothing to it. I'd done a film, Croupier, where I'd worn a tuxedo and there was nothing more than that. Playing James Bond would have been like entering a golden prison, and I doubt that would have suited me. I never understood what I would have been able to add to the role, or how I could play a character who has already been defined in the past. For me, Sean Connery is the real James Bond."

As for Hugh Jackman, he was in his mid thirties and had become a breakout star and instant leading man after his charismatic turn as Wolverine in the first X-Men film. Jackman could have been a terrific Bond and was clearly on the radar of EON. Jackman's agent was sounded out about Bond in 2002 and asked if his client would be interested in the role. However, Jackman rather recoiled at the invitation. He was about to start shooting X-Men 2 and with offers flooding in and his career starting to take off in a big way, Jackman (rather like Clive Owen or Jude Law) simply didn't want to constrict himself to a franchise like Bond. "I sort of have (been asked)," said Jackman concerning James Bond. "At the time I was just about to do X-Men 2 and I was like, Ah, I don't think it's the right time. But it was not an easy one to give up. I just felt at the time that the scripts had become so unbelievable and crazy, and I felt like they needed to become grittier and real. And the response was: 'Oh, you don't get a say. You just have to sign on.' I was also worried that between Bond and X-Men, I'd never have time to do different things."

Another fairly obvious person to look at for James Bond was Christian Bale. Bale was about thirty years at the time and starting to establish himself as a leading man through films like Equilibrium and Reign of Fire. According to the book Christian Bale: The Inside Story of the Darkest Batman, Barbara Broccoli was much taken with Bale's performance as Patrick Batemen in the film version of American Psycho and would happily have cast him as Bond. It's obviously difficult to know how much truth there was in this and - besides - Barbara already had her heart set on Daniel Craig by the time that serious casting began to replace Pierce Brosnan.

Around this time, Christian Bale made some disparaging comments about the Bond franchise (he thought Bond represented 'every despicable stereotype about England and British actors' - whatever that is supposed to mean) and plainly wasn't interested in the part. In an interview with Esquire some time later Bale was asked about Bond and said no one at EON ever approached him about the role. By the time of Casino Royale, Christian Bale already had a franchise of his own playing Batman for Christopher Nolan. Bale was actually very James Bondish as Bruce Wayne - especially in Batman Begins. You can easily picture the Bale of Batman Begins as James Bond.

In 2004, Pierce Brosnan said that his fellow Irish actor Colin Farrell should replace him as Bond - which naturally led to much media speculation that Farrell was going to be the new 007. Colin Farrell was about 28 at the time. Though handsome and a very good actor it's debatable if Farrell was right for Bond. It was all moot anyway because he wasn't interested and there is no evidence that the producers were interested in him. Farrell had work coming out of his ears at the time and seemed to be in virtually every film that came out so it's not as if he needed Bond. He had a great career already. "The idea of me playing James Bond got into the press, but it is not true and I would not like to do it," said Farrell. "They should find someone the audience has no history with."

Another young Irish actor who was linked to the part of Bond in the media at this time was Stuart Townsend. He was 31 and had appeared in films like The League of Extraordinary Gentlemen and Queen of the Damned. There isn't much evidence though that Townsend was ever a real contender. Stuart Townsend once had a very promising career ahead of him but it seemed to fizzle out very quickly. He was cast as Aragorn in Peter Jackson's Lord of the Rings but then fired and replaced by Viggo Mortensen at the last minute just as shooting began. This experience understandably seemed to leave Townsend rather bitter and disillusioned with the film industry.

It was reported that Joseph Fiennes was contacted about playing Bond in the preamble to Casino Royale but had no interest in the part. He was the younger brother of Ralph Fiennes and a successful actor in his own right. Joseph Fiennes, who was about 35, had been in films like Shakespeare in Love and probably thought Bond was slightly beneath him or something he didn't need - though having said that Fiennes was in Rancid Aluminium in 2000 and many think that might be the WORST British film ever made. Maybe Joseph Fiennes thought he simply wasn't right for Bond. In recent years you may have seen Joseph Fiennes playing Fred Waterford in The Handmaid's Tale.

Ioan Gruffudd said he had a meeting with Barbara Broccoli to discuss playing James Bond circa 2004. Gruffudd was best known for his portrayal of Horatio Hornblower in the Hornblower series of television films. Though on the face of it a decent shout for 007 and about the right age, Gruffudd could not be considered because he was simply unavailable. "Whenever it comes up, my name is associated," said Gruffud, "I'll be honest, I did have a meeting with Barbara Broccoli, but it was around the same time that I'd literally just got cast as Mr Fantastic. I was impossible to tender for another franchise at the time."

Dominic West appears to have been in vague contention for Casino Royale at some point or other. He was about 35 and playing Detective Jimmy McNulty in the highly acclaimed television show The Wire. West was an Old Etonian and had recently appeared in films like Mona Lisa Smile and Chicago. Dominic West claims that he turned up to his interview in a pair of jeans to distinguish himself from the other sharp suited contenders and further claimed that he withdrew himself from contention in the end. It's hard to know what to make of West's attitude to Bond or how seriously he was considered. West always looked a trifle too stereotypically posh to be a believably tough Bond but fans of The Wire might disagree. Pointless trivia - several years later West played the infamous British serial killer Fred West in a television drama.

Matthew Goode was definitely someone who was considered for Casino Royale. He was still in his twenties and had just appeared in the films Chasing Liberty and Match Point. Goode has confirmed that he was one of the candidates to replace Brosnan. Goode is one of those British actors who is rather typecast as a period toff but he did get to play Ozymandias in Zack Snyder's adaptation of Watchmen. Goode seems a little slight to be Bond but would have been suave and polished in the role had it come his way. Goode is 43 at the time of writing so it appears that Casino Royale was his one and only chance to be Bond.

Sam Heughan auditioned to play Bond for Casino Royale. He was in his mid twenties at the time and had few screen credits so one might presume that his stage work got him noticed. In 2021, Heughan said - "I went up for it when they did Bond 21. It was an amazing experience and I was completely out of my depth. But I think now I feel the right age for it, I feel capable enough to do it, I'd love the opportunity to throw my hat in the ring." Heughan would be best known later for the TV show Outlander. Heughan is one of those actors who never stops talking about how he'd like to be the next Bond - which is a tactic that never quite seems to work. It's probably best to be coy! It seems doubtful that Sam Heughan will get another crack at Bond now. Next time around they are likely (you would think) to be looking for a younger actor in his twenties or thirties and Heughan has aged out of that demographic now.

Cristian Solimeno was interviewed about the role of Bond in Casino Royale. Solimeno was about thirty years-old and best known for his role in the television show Footballer's Wives. He had a decent enough look for Bond in that he had black hair and was quite handsome. Solimeno has remained a very busy actor with most of his credits coming on television. A few years after his Bond interview Solimeno featured in a Highlander television movie with Adrian Paul. Daniel Goddard was also a candidate for Casino Royale although he is not believed to have got very deep into the casting sessions. Goddard was 34, Australian, and from 1999 to 2002 played the lead role in the television fantasy show Beastmaster. Goddard looked the part and was no stranger to stunts and action but one must presume his acting was deemed to be not quite up to the standard they were looking for. In 2007,

Goddard began a very long stint on the American soap opera The Young and the Restless.

Numerous media sources named Steven Brand as someone on the radar of EON in 2005. Brand was a 36 year-old Scottish actor who had recently appeared in the Hollywood film The Scorpion King. Brand was definitely on a long list of Bond candidates but he doesn't seem to have been involved in the final shake up. His film career never really went anywhere in the end (Brand seems to have made several low-budget horror films) but he has appeared in big TV shows like NCIS: Los Angeles, Hawaii Five-0, and Alex Rider. Brand looks a bit like a dark haired version of Sean Pertwee.

Martin Campbell had a meeting with Ingo Rademacher to discuss the part of Bond during the Casino Royale sweepstakes. Rademacher was in his mid thirties and blond and good looking. He was born in Germany and grew up in Australia before becoming a soap star in the United States. It's hard to imagine that Rademacher was ever a very serious candidate. Another Australian candidate was alleged to be 25 year-old Heath Ledger. Despite his youth, Ledger was already establishing himself as a highly promising film actor thanks to pictures like The Four Feathers and A Knight's Tale. Although EON may have been interested in Ledger it is claimed that he wasn't interested in Bond because he feared it would typecast him. Ledger sadly died far too young in 2008 not long after after his brilliant performance as the Joker in The Dark Knight.

The Bond casting circus always has a tabloid silly season where a few ludicrous names or mistaken theories are dropped into the mix and Casino Royale was certainly no different. The newspapers made a big deal of the pop star Robbie Williams gunning for the part of Bond but Williams had about as much chance of becoming James Bond as Eddie Edwards did of winning the Olympic ski-jump. The American musical theatre star Rikki Lee Travolta was often cited as a Bond candidate around this time but there was no truth to these stories at all.

"I had agreed to do a cameo appearance in a film called Crime Fiction," said Travolta, "and a few days after filming my scene, a story appeared on the Internet that I had been summoned from the set of Crime Fiction to fly to England to shoot a screen test for James Bond. Nothing of the sort had happened. I had never even been contacted for a screen test for Bond, much less having executed one. Suddenly, there were countless press releases claiming to be from my manager on my being courted to be the next Bond. None of that was true, the press releases were totally fabricated and not from my camp at all."

The 47 year-old Scottish actor Ewan Stewart was named by a number of sources as a Bond candidate in 2004 and 2005. His age alone should have made people realise the story was bogus. Stewart had actually been hired by EON to play the villain against prospective Bond actors in auditions and this led to everyone getting their wires crossed and wrongly assuming that Stewart had auditioned for Bond. "The truth is I was never in the running," said Stewart. "In fact they wanted someone to read opposite the potential Bonds. They had an assortment of people going through the audition process, there were two days of full-on screen tests and they needed an actor to read the part of the baddie. And somehow word gets out that I'm up for the part. I just pretended it was a serious consideration. Why not? Who wouldn't want to be Bond?"

A 36 year-old Irish actor called Chris Feeney claimed that he got to the final round of auditions for Casino Royale - though this seems highly unlikely to say the least. He only had a couple of credits at the time - an appearance in an Irish TV show and a small part in a short film about LSD. Feeney apparently served with the armed forces in the United States and claimed to be a real life action man who was an expert sniper and had done more parachute jumps than you've had hot dinners. Chris Feeney always felt more like a very inventive publicist for himself rather than a genuine Bond candidate. He was only 5'9 and looked nothing like Bond in the few available pictures of him online.

Three New Zealand actors were looked at by EON for Casino Royale. The first of these was 30 year-old Martin Henderson. Henderson was handsome (in a slightly bland Tom Cruise sort of way) and had just appeared in the action film Torque. He was also in the 2002 Hollywood remake of the Japanese horror film The Ring and the well regarded 2005 Australian film Little Fish. Henderson does not appear to have become a serious contender for the part of James Bond in Casino Royale though. It could be that Henderson's height didn't help as he's only 5'9. The second actor from New Zealand under consideration was Antony Starr. Starr was a stronger candidate than Henderson. He was was 31 and had just shot a film called The World's Fastest Indian with Anthony Hopkins. Though a pretty good Bond candidate, Starr does not appear to have made it into the final rounds of contention. Starr is best known these days for playing the villainous superhero Homelander in The Boys.

The third New Zealander was Karl Urban. Urban met with the Bond producers to discuss the 007 role for Casino Royale. He was in his early thirties and appearing in the Lord of the Rings franchise at the time in addition to The Bourne Supremacy and Chronicles of Riddick. He was fast becoming a very prolific film actor. Urban said he couldn't do a Bond audition in the end because he was simply too busy. "Yeah, there was a period when they were casting it the last time around where I'd met with Barbara Broccoli and various other producers," said Urban in 2016. "Unfortunately I was shooting another movie and I couldn't do the final test. I'm actually pretty grateful I didn't because I think Daniel Craig did such an extraordinary job and I couldn't have imagined a better Bond." Karl Urban didn't really need James Bond and has enjoyed a busy and fantastic career thanks to things like Dredd, The Boys, and Star Trek.

Matthew Macfadyen seemed to suggest in 2005 that he had been in contact with the Bond producers concerning the 007 gig. Macfadyen was 30 years-old and best known for his role in the spy themed television show Spooks. In 2005 he had one of his most famous roles when he played Mr Darcy in a film version of Pride and Prejudice. Macfadyen doesn't seem to have been a very serious candidate for Casino Royale. It's debatable if he looked the part and there were probably plenty of better candidates. "I don't know about Bond," said Macfadyen at the time. "It's a weird one, isn't it? It's a bit camp. It would change your life" These days Macfadyen is probably best known for appearing in the TV show Succession.

Another star of the TV show Spooks linked to Bond was Rupert Penry-Jones. Penry-Jones was about 34 at the time and for a brief window was actually the favourite with some bookies. He was blond but that obviously wouldn't have bothered the producers because Daniel Craig was cast in the end. Rupert Penry-Jones was one of those actors who made no secret of the fact that he'd love to play Bond but it doesn't appear that he was ever in serious contention for Casino Royale. He was later in the TV show Whitechapel and in 2008 played Richard Hannay in a BBC television film version of The 39 Steps.

Luke Mably was a young British actor who auditioned to be Bond in Casino Royale. Mably had recently had roles in The Prince & Me (a romcom in which Mably played a Prince who romances Julia Stiles) and Danny Boyle's 28 Days Later. Mably was about 28 at the time of his Bond audition. He does not appear to have become a serious candidate. Although he never really became a big star Mably showed some decent acting chops in the 2009 horror film Exam and has appeared in high profile TV shows like NCIS: New Orleans and Seal Team. Mably was probably still a bit too boyish in 2004 to be a credible Bond candidate. He has done all sorts since his Bond audition. He was even in one of those Rise of the Footsoldier gangster films.

Geraint Owen, who was about 38 at the time, attended more than one reading concerning the part of James Bond in Casino Royale. Owen was an actor in the Welsh-language soap Pobol y Cwm. "I got a call from my agent who said I'd better get to Tunbridge Wells and he told me it was the first audition for the part of James Bond," said Owen at the time. "It was one hell of a drive and I didn't really have to do any lines when I got there." Owen was later a councillor for Plaid Cymru. He tragically died in 2009 after suffering a brain haemorrhage. It's hard to say if Geraint Owen would have been a credible Bond. You'd probably have had to watch Pobol y Cwm to know as he didn't do much else.

Roderick O'Grady was another largely unknown actor who read for the part of Bond in Casino Royale. O'Grady was from Northern Ireland and known primarily for his stage work. He had a mildly Bondish look though he wasn't the most handsome 007 candidate you've ever seen. O'Grady's agent let slip that he had read for the part of Bond. O'Grady had few screen credits - an appearance in The Bill being the most notable. O'Grady turned his hand to writing after his brush with James Bond and hasn't acted much since 2005. In 2019 though he did appear in the television show Pennyworth.

Tristan Gemmill has said that he was interviewed about playing Bond in Casino Royale. He was in his early to mid thirties and had appeared in British television shows like Eastenders and The Bill. Gemmill was later best known for his role as Robert Preston in the soap opera Coronation Street. You can't really imagine that Gemmill got very advanced in the casting process. There were plenty of better candidates. "I auditioned for James Bond before Daniel Craig," said Gemmill. "They saw pretty much every actor in England who could walk upright. I met the casting director and between us on her desk were piles of DVDs of Ewan McGregor movies, Jude Law movies and Hugh Jackman movies. I could barely see her over this pile of DVDs. So what chance did I stand in that company?"

The former boxer turned actor Gary Stretch appears to have been in some sort of contention for the 007 role in Casino Royale. The British tabloids at the time often reported that

Stretch had been called back to do more tests and interviews. Stretch was 36 years-old and the former British junior-middleweight champion. He was something of a glamour boy in British boxing and supplemented his income by working as a model. In 1991 he challenged Chris Eubank for WBO middleweight championship but was stopped in a bad-tempered and messy fight. Stretch had been acting since 1994 and featured in the film Final Combination with Michael Madsen and Lisa Bonet that same year. Stretch earned good reviews for his role as a scuzzy drug dealer in the cult 2004 Shane Meadows film Dead Men's Shoes and then had a role in the Oliver Stone film Alexander. Gary Stretch was actually not a bad actor at all and got a lot further in the Bond sweepstakes than his fellow former boxer Glenn McCrory did in 1994. Stretch's acting career didn't fufil its early promise though and in 2010 he suffered the indignity of appearing in Mega Shark Versus Crocosaurus.

The Australian actor Julian McMahon was a popular Bond candidate around the time that Casino Royale was being cast. He was 36 and best known for playing the ladies man Christian Troy in the TV show Nip/Tuck. At the start of 2005, McMahon was quoted as saying - "I met the producers for a final audition. They told me to expect a decision in a couple of months and they said it was between me and one other person." In a curious subplot, McMahon's mother told the press he had turned down Bond because of his television contract. Another theory is that McMahon couldn't be considered for Bond because he had taken the role of villain Dr Doom in the Fantastic Four franchise (which only amounted to two forgettable films in the end) and was unavailable. In more recent years McMahon has said he auditioned for Casino Royale but whether he got as close to the part as he makes out is impossible to know.

Alex O'Loughlin (at the time billed as Alex O'Lachlan) was a serious candidate for Casino Royale. The Australian actor was about 28 and had just made his film debut in the drama film The Oyster Farmer. O'Loughlin was tall, black haired, good looking, and a fairly tough looking chap. He seemed to be a very good 007 candidate. "I met with Martin Campbell here in Los Angeles at his office on the Sony lot," said O'Loughlin at the time, "and he asked me to fly to London and test and we tested at Pinewood. I was fitted out at Hugo Boss for a tuxedo, had my hair cut and filmed two scenes. It's James Bond, need I say any more? The reality is I may not get the role, which is the conundrum for all actors, but at the end of the day, I'm incredibly grateful just to be considered."

The casting directors claimed it was Alex O'Loughlin's age which nixed his chances of playing Bond (which I don't quite get myself because Lazenby was a similar age in OHMSS and Connery was only thirtyish when he became Bond). In the book A Star is Found: Our Adventures Casting Some of Hollywood's Biggest Movies, the casting directors on Casino Royale said of Alex O'Loughlin - "We were all very excited about Alex O'Loughlin, for example, partly because he was so young. Alex is a terrifically sexy, masterful, and take-charge person - just the type who can make you remember that James Bond is a seriously dangerous man. He might make a fabulous Bond in a few years, but when we saw him, he just didn't seem old enough for that 007 sense of command." Alex O'Loughlin has done a lot of television work since his Bond audition - most famously as the lead in Hawaii Five-0.

One of the strongest candidates EON found for Casino Royale was Rupert Friend. Friend was in his early twenties and had just made his film debut in the Johnny Depp film The Libertine. Debbie McWilliams, the Bond casting director, liked Rupert Friend and thought he was an exceptional candidate. Friend was dark-haired and good looking and with a bit of weight training could have been a good Bond. Friend rather recoiled at the interest in him though because of his age and decided not to pursue the role. "I just thought, 'I'm too young for this. I need to have some life experience. James Bond needs to have lived," said Friend. "I love Bond films. I don't want to be the person who messes it up because he hasn't got miles on the clock." Years later Friend would become best

known for playing CIA action man Peter Quinn in the
Showtime political thriller series Homeland.

Martin Campbell managed to persuade EON to audition Goran
Višnjic for Casino Royale. Višnjic was a 32 year-old Croatian
actor who portrayed Dr Luka Kovač in the medical drama ER.
It is believed that Campbell was impressed by the actor when
Višnjic unsuccessfully auditioned for the lead role in
Campbell's Zorro movie. Višnjic spoke perfect English and did
an impressive test. He was dark-haired and very handsome. In
fact, it is believed that Višnjic was so good he got to the final
four candidates. If Daniel Craig had been kidnapped by aliens
then Višnjic might well have had a plausible shot at bagging
the part. According to the casting director Debbie McWilliams
though, Višnjic was deemed too young to get the part in the
end. This (again) feels like an odd thing to say because Višnjic
was only about five years younger than Daniel Craig and
hardly looked like a little boy. If you watch ER from this era
Goran Višnjic looks perfectly adult and grown-up!

In the end, after all the endless interviews, readings, and
auditions, only three men were left standing. One of these
three men would be James Bond but one candidate in
particular had a distinct advantage over the others in that he
was the personal choice of Barbara Broccoli. That candidate
was of course Daniel Craig.

Daniel Craig was 37 years-old and had appeared in many
films. His roles included Tomb Raider, (Ted Hughes in) Sylvia,
Road to Perdition, Layer Cake, and Enduring Love. Daniel
Craig was genuinely perplexed and baffled when he was first
contacted by EON and asked if he'd like to do a James Bond
screen test. He was a million miles away from the traditional
tall, dark, handsome Bond template. Craig thought that the
Bond people must have gone mad. Barbara Broccoli assured
him though that she was deadly serious and wanted him to do
an audition. She told Craig that if he got the part he could do it
in his own way. He wouldn't have to copy or mimic any of the
Bond actors that had gone before.

Craig said he was very reluctant at first to pursue the part of Bond but eventually decided to go for it and do a test. At the time he was shooting a sci-fi movie called The Invasion with Nicole Kidman and had to fly back to Britain to do a test at Pinewood. Craig had long hair at his screen test because he was in the middle of shooting a movie and obviously couldn't get his hair cut. Truth be told, Craig was the only person Barbara Broccoli wanted for Bond. If it was up to her they wouldn't have tested anyone else. However, the studio and Martin Campbell were not entirely convinced by Daniel Craig and so other options (much to Barbara's irritation you'd imagine) had been explored.

Craig's main competition for the part of James Bond in Casino Royale, once the long list of potential actors had been whittled down by numerous interviews, readings, auditions, and screen tests, was a fairly unknown young English born Australian actor named Sam Worthington and a completely unknown 22 year-old actor from the Channel Islands named Henry Cavill. Sam Worthington was thirty years-old and had appeared in films like Hart's War and Somersault. He was seen as someone who was very much a rising star. Worthington wasn't the most obviously Bondian person in terms of his looks but he was good looking all the same and young enough to throw himself into all the stunts and action.

"They (EON) had seen my tapes and wanted to make Bond younger, like (Matt Damon in) The Bourne Identity," said Worthington. "So they kept phoning up, wanting me to audition, but I kept refusing." Worthington was eventually persuaded though to do a screen test for Martin Campbell. "I read every single book, saw every film I could and did everything to prepare myself," said Worthington. "I wasn't wasting anyone's time; I gave it the best I could. I think it's amazingly good-going to get where I did. I gave it a damn good crack."

It is clear that Sam Worthington got to the final round of

auditions and had Daniel Craig removed himself from contention it is highly possible that Worthington would have got the part. Not long after his 007 audition, Worthington had an incredible run where he appeared in huge films like Terminator Salvation, Clash of the Titans, and Avatar. Losing out on Bond had no negative effect on Worthington's career at all. Worthington continues to be a busy actor and will be seen in the Avatar sequels. Though he has had a great career, some critics think Worthington is a rather bland actor who probably wouldn't have made a great 007. It's all academic now anyway. We'll never know how Worthington would have fared had he been cast as Bond.

Henry Cavill only had a few credits (which included the film The Count of Monte Cristo) to his name at time of Casino Royale's casting. He had though a close brush with stardom in 2003 when the director McG cast him as Superman. However, McG left the film and was replaced as director by Bryan Singer. Singer cast Brandon Routh as Superman instead. Cavill is often alleged to have been the runner up when it came to casting Bond in Casino Royale. He was definitely in there with a chance until the bitter end. "Martin Campbell and I both enjoyed Henry Cavill's audition," said the 007 composer David Arnold, who provided music for the Casino Royale screen test footage. "He had all the swagger and physicality but maybe, as he was in his early twenties, felt just a little bit too young. We thought he had great presence and we weren't at all surprised when he turned into Superman."

It is often reported that Martin Campbell wanted to cast Henry Cavill as Bond rather than Daniel Craig. It's impossible to know how true this story is but it would provide an explanation for why Campbell seemed a trifle grumpy at the press conference which unveiled Craig as Bond! "Perhaps Henry Cavill was too young for it then, he was 22 at the time we auditioned for Casino Royale, but maybe he could still be James Bond in the future," Martin Campbell later said. "After all, Pierce Brosnan did a great screen test only to eventually get the part years later." When it became known that Henry

Cavill was in contention to play Bond there were rumours that Pierce Brosnan was going to come back to do Casino Royale and Cavill was going to play the younger version of Brosnan's Bond in flashbacks! These rumours were obviously nonsense. Brosnan was history.

Henry Cavill was the most handsome of the Casino Royale candidates. There is no doubt that he looked like James Bond. Not long after his audition he was in the TV show The Tudors and in 2011 he was cast as Superman in the film Man of Steel. His status as the nearly man of Hollywood was finally put to bed. Cavill became a star in his own right. He has often spoken about his dream to play James Bond one day but it could be that 2005 was his one and only chance. "At this stage, it's all up in the air. We'll see what happens. But yes, I would love to play Bond, it would be very, very exciting," Cavill told GQ in 2020. "If Barbara and Michael were interested in that, I would absolutely jump at the opportunity."

The reaction to Daniel Craig's casting in 2005 was underwhelming. Most people had never heard of him. Craig gave a poor impression at his first press conference by chewing gum and not displaying much in the way of personality. The Sun called him James Bland. Barbara Broccoli and Michael G Wilson were dismayed by the negative press.

A website (which still exists) was set up to protest at his casting. The website complained that Craig was 'short, craggy, and blond' and looked more like Putin than James Bond. You could say that Daniel Craig had the last laugh though. Casino Royale was a tremendous critical success and 2012's Skyfall was a huge financial blockbuster. There was never any background noise during Craig's first three films about other Bond contenders. In fact, Barbara Broccoli was open about her desire for Craig to play Bond forever. It was only after the 2015 film Spectre that the old familiar 007 background rumblings began again.

SPECULATION AFTER SPECTRE

Daniel Craig, famously, made some ill-advised off the cuff comments at the end of the Spectre shoot when he said he would rather 'slash his own wrists' than make another Bond film. This was clearly a stupid (not to mention offensive) thing to say and a consequence of being tired and sore after an exhausting six month shoot. Craig, in mitigation for his comments, would later say that he shot Spectre in constant pain because of a leg injury he suffered during the production. He'd also spent close to a year away from home and his family completing his commitments to the film (a Bond actor is obviously required to do extensive stunt training before the film and extensive publicity to promote the film after it is completed). Craig had even doubled down on the wrist-slashing comments though by declaring that he would only make another Bond film for the money.

Of course, actors are not paid in jelly beans. They, like everyone, desire money. Even so, it was a fairly classless thing for Daniel Craig to say. It suggested that Craig's only connection to the Bond films was his salary and that he didn't care about them at all. This was clearly not the case because he worked ferociously hard on the Bond films and took a great interest in the production and creative decisions. Craig's interview after Spectre was a classic foot in mouth moment on every level. He really wasn't thinking at all. One can only imagine the reaction of studio executives when they read Craig's comments. He came across as ungrateful and charmless.

Though never officially confirmed by anyone, there was a general perception at the time of its release that Spectre would probably be the last Daniel Craig Bond film. His comments in that unfortunate interview were obviously a big factor in this perception (as was Craig's reported participation in a 20 episode Showtime TV show called Purity - which didn't actually get made in the end) but there was also a strong sense

that Spectre, whatever its faults, did serve as a reasonable way
to put the lid on the Craig era and give his version of Bond a
fairly definitive (and happy) sort of ending. It was hard really
to see how much more could be mined out of the loose
continuity of the Craig films. Maybe it was time for the
franchise to undertake a soft reboot and head in a different
direction. What had been different and bold in the Craig era
for a couple of films was in danger of becoming stale and
tiresome after four movies.

The media love nothing more than speculating on who the
next James Bond will be and the man who emerged as the
favourite in this uncertain 2015/2016 period of doubt over
Craig's future participation in the franchise was Tom
Hiddleston. Hiddleston, best known as Loki in the Marvel
films, had turned in a vaguely Bondish performance in the
BBC miniseries The Night Manager. This was enough for
rumours to abound, with some degree of certainty, that trusted
sources had suggested Hiddleston had done a successful
screen test (directed by Sam Mendes no less) and would be
unveiled as the new James Bond by the end of 2016. Those
who are familiar with forums and entertainment websites will
have learned by now that the phrase 'from a trusted source' is
to be taken with a dose of salt considerably larger than a pinch.

The Hiddleston stories came thick and fast but they were
never consistent and they were never verified. One magazine
claimed Hiddleston had been seen cosily chatting with
Barbara Broccoli in an exclusive London gentleman's club.
Another magazine said Broccoli disliked Tom Hiddleston
because she found him too smug. The tabloids said Hiddleston
had blown his chances because of his bizarre 'PR romance'
with Taylor Swift. Even the veteran thriller writer Frederick
Forsyth decided, for reasons best known to himself!, to add his
two pence to the speculation. "I got a tip the other day which
I'll share with you," he told the Sunday Mail. "I understand
Barbara Broccoli is absolutely no way going to pick Tom
Hiddleston. No. Way." It was Hiddleston himself who poured
cold water on the speculation. Hiddleston said that no one had

approached him about playing Bond in the first place and we shouldn't hold our breath waiting for an announcement.

The tabloids then alleged that EON had a meeting with Tom Hardy to discuss him playing 007 while it was still uncertain if Daniel Craig was coming back as Bond. Furthermore, they claimed that there was a big 'beef' between Hardy and Craig and that the meeting was designed to 'prompt' Craig's immediate return because he would surely not want to see his great hated rival Tom Hardy replace him. The idea that Daniel Craig and Tom Hardy were like a modern day feuding Bette Davis and Joan Crawford was of course completely unsubstantiated and suspiciously speculative. It would certainly not be the last time though that Tom Hardy would be linked to the part of James Bond (even as the Daniel Craig era rumbled on with no clear end in sight).

When the media speculate who the next Bond might be they sometimes throw a few actresses into the mix as if James Bond is suddenly going to become Jane Bond. This would be as stupid as Lara Croft becoming Larry Croft. This recent speculation about a gender switch was probably inspired by Jodie Whittaker becoming the first female lead in Doctor Who. However, the Doctor is a regenerating alien. There is a plausible (as far as a sci-fi show can be plausible) explanation for why the Doctor (having previously been male) is now a woman. There is no such explanation for why James Bond should suddenly become a woman. Barbara Broccoli shot this speculation down in flames herself when she said that Bond would always be a man and she would prefer that new interesting roles for women were created rather than male characters become female.

The tabloid silly season when it came to casting the next James Bond continued all through the development and production of Daniel Craig's final bow No Time To Die. Jamie Bell, James Norton, Michael Fassbender, and Aiden Turner were all at various points anointed as the heir apparent and the favoured son of Barbara Broccoli at different stages of

Bond 25's genesis and production. It is certainly true that EON are always on the look out for actors with Bond potential. It would be no surprise if Barbara Broccoli had made a mental note (for future reference) of some young British actor she had noticed in something. However, the idea that EON had cast the next Bond while the paint from the Craig era wasn't even dry yet was patently absurd. The next James Bond actor was something that Broccoli didn't even want to think about until such time as it became an absolute necessity.

The concept of the 'reserve Bond' did not exist in the Barbara Broccoli era. She refused to even contemplate anyone other than Daniel Craig playing Bond and was always willing to wait for as long it took between films for Craig to decide if he wanted to come back or not. There was definitely no plan B in the Barbara Broccoli era. There were rumours that Barbara liked particular actors and kept them in mind (it was alleged a few years ago, for example, that Barbara is quite keen on Jack Huston for Bond) but you can bet your life that none of them were flown to the locations of Daniel Craig films and given a costume fitting. Trying to predict who the next Bond might be is a precarious task because the landscape is always shifting. The next Bond actor could easily be someone why doesn't presently show up on any next 007 list radar.

While Bond 25 had not even started shooting, the tabloids had already started casting the next Bond themselves. It was reported that, on the back of the success of the BBC miniseries The Bodyguard, Richard Madden had met Barbara Broccoli and been offered the part of James Bond in Bond 26. This was news to Madden and Broccoli. "It's very flattering to be involved in that conversation at all," said Madden, "but it's all just talk, and I'm sure next week it'll be someone different." Even Danny Boyle, who was originally supposed to direct Bond 25, joined in with the armchair 007 casting games and suggested that Robert Pattinson should be the next Bond. An interesting suggestion but - alas - Pattinson was to become Batman thus (you would presume) making him an unlikely candidate.

One of the more fanciful stories during the wait for No Time To Die was that the pop star Harry Styles was gunning to replace Daniel Craig and also planned to sing the theme song to his own movie. While this would be a first the chances of it happening were rather remote. Harry Styles did appear in Christopher Nolan's Dunkirk and didn't do a bad job at all but you probably wouldn't want to put any money on him becoming the next 007.

No Time to Die hadn't even reached its next projected release date when the Bond silly season began again in earnest. A number of newspapers latched onto a new unverified website report that Tom Hardy had signed a deal to replace Daniel Craig and would be unveiled as the new 007 at the end of 2020. Putting aside the fact that, at 43, Hardy was plainly on the old side to be kickstarting the next era of Bond (at the rate EON make films these days, Hardy would have been an old age pensioner by the time he got to his third adventure!), it was surely unrealistic to believe that EON had cast the new Bond before the last film featuring the old Bond had even come out! Still, if nothing else, the Tom Hardy story proved that the search for the next Bond is one of those games we never tire of.

The Daniel Craig era has been festooned with silly tabloid and entertainment website rumours that Idris Elba will be the next Bond - and the first black Bond to boot. While no one doubts that Elba is an excellent actor who has proved himself as a commanding and charismatic leading man the problem with these rumours is that Elba is only about three or four years younger than Daniel Craig. What would be the point in replacing Daniel Craig with someone who was nearly as old as he was? It would be completely pointless. Elba would be as old as Roger Moore in A View To A Kill by the time he made a couple of Bond films! The danger with the next Bond guessing game is that viable candidates under the microscope are gradually replaced by new contenders. A particular actor you had in mind might get too old for the part before it comes around again. Or he might not be interested anyway. Then you have the X-Factor of Barbara Broccoli. We don't really know who is on her private radar.

The frustrating thing for modern Bond candidates is that Daniel Craig's last movie took six years to actually reach the screen after Spectre. When you factor in the understandable need for EON to take a breather after No Time To Die and not rush into their next iteration of James Bond, this means you can add another two or three (maybe even more knowing EON!) years before the next film is cast and enters production. If one were casting a new Bond in 2016 you would have some fairly viable youngish candidates like Dan Stevens, Tom Hiddleston, and Aiden Turner all ready to go. However those actors will be in their forties by the time cameras on the next film begin rolling.

The long drawn out nature of Craig's last film (the latter delays due to COVID were obviously not EON's fault but they definitely could and should have made this film sooner than they actually did in the end) may have aged a generation of 007 candidates out of contention and opened the door to a fresh younger batch of 007 wannabes. That's the unavoidable nature of the Bond casting circus. It's impossible to predict what the situation might look like in a few years.

EPILOGUE

The Daniel Craig era finally drew to a close with No Time To Die in 2021. It's fair to say that the Craig era became preposterously elongated in the end. It is difficult not to have sympathy with Bond fans who wish that the process of making these films could be accelerated somewhat so that the gaps between movies were much less frustrating. Long gaps between films is something that never used to happen in the Bond series (aside from a famously frustrating and long hiatus between 1989 and 1995 - which was due to litigation over TV rights and nothing to do with the producers or lead actor wanting a break).

Roger Moore made seven Bond films between 1973 and 1985. Timothy Dalton had two Bond adventures out in the space of two years. Pierce Brosnan's Bond films arrived in 1995, 1997, 1999, and 2002. It was only with the Daniel Craig era of Bond that production of these movies became what you might describe as sporadic. Quantum of Solace, in the Bond tradition, arrived in 2008 - two years after Casino Royale. It was after Quantum that the frustration began. Bond fans then had to wait four years for the next entry - Skyfall. Fans then had to wait three years for Spectre. Fans were then expected to wait FIVE years for Bond 25 - until the coronavirus made this wait even longer. The gaps between Bond films in the Craig era had become far too long.

One must hope that one change in the Bond franchise going forward is a more regular schedule when it comes to movies. Amazon acquiring a stake in MGM may or may not make this happen. Money will certainly be no problem now so it's just a question of whether EON are capable of going back to the old Cubby days when Bond films were a regular thing and not just something that occurred once in a blue moon. Cubby Broccoli would not have sat on his thumbs for two years waiting for a Bond actor to decide if he wanted to come back or not in the way that Barbara Broccoli did with Daniel Craig and Bond 25. Cubby would have simply recast the part and got the cameras rolling again. No actor was bigger than the Bond franchise.

Now that the Craig era is finally consigned to the past the next task facing EON is to find a replacement. That will require many interviews, auditions, readings, screen tests.

It will also be the subject of inevitable silly tabloid and entertainment website gossip and speculation. And you know what? That's all part of the fun. Many years from now the story of how EON found Daniel Craig's replacement will be told and what a tale it will be. Pop stars who have never so much as acted in a school play will be erroneously put on the candidate shortlist by tabloids. Actors who played bad tempered bearded small businessmen in Emmerdale and Hollyoaks will regale us with tales of how they read for the part and got really (honestly) close to being picked. A man with no IMDB credits to his name aside from Megacrocogoldfish v Giantoctopus will tell us on his website that he got to the final four and bumped into Aiden Turner in the toilets at Pinewood Studios.

As we have seen in this book, trying to predict who the next Bond will be is a rather foolhardy mission. No one back in 2002 would have guessed that Daniel Craig would be playing Bond in the next film. It's probably debatable that anyone would have predicted in 1985 that Timothy Dalton would be Roger Moore's replacement. When it comes to the next Bond actor you should probably expect the unexpected. The Bond franchise is one of the few examples of a huge mainstream movie where it doesn't really matter who the leading man is. You don't need to hire a star because James Bond IS the star. No one knew Sean Connery from Adam when he was cast as Bond. Daniel Craig was hardly a household name when he got the part. Pierce Brosnan was making television movies when he was cast as Bond. The only actor who had a reasonably high profile going into Bond was Roger Moore - thanks to his television shows The Saint and The Persuaders. Roger was most definitely not a film star though at the time and had no track record to speak of when it came to opening a movie with his mere presence.

The recasting of the lead actor naturally gives the Bond franchise a temporary injection of freshness and novelty. Goldeneye and Casino Royale were both evidence of this. The Living Daylights (whatever anyone might try to retrospectively tell you about the Timothy Dalton era) was also very well received in 1987. A Bond film that marks the debut of a new lead actor is always hugely anticipated. My choice for the next Bond would be Aiden Turner - who had classic Dalton looks and vibes in And Then There Were None. I think Nicholas Hoult has excellent Bond potential too and might be an interesting choice. There is no doubt that Henry Cavill would be a fantastic looking Bond but would he be too obvious a choice now? Naturally though I won't be placing a bet. No doubt I've put the mockers on all of these candidates simply by mentioning them. Part of the intrigue of Bond casting is that you never quite know who you might end up with.

There is of course always a chance too that the next Bond might be someone that many of us have barely heard of. This is something that I would actually welcome. I love the idea of taking a young actor we hardly know and turning him into Bond. EON haven't really done that since Lazenby in OHMSS. In the modern era of Bond with Barbara Broccoli all bets are basically off when it comes to Bond casting. She is unlikely to choose the most obvious person. This will make the next 007 casting an intriguing prospect. The post-Craig era will be a fascinating crossroads for this venerable franchise.

The biggest problem facing Bond 26 is not really the leading man though. You should be able to find any number of actors who could make a decent fist of playing 007 and look good in a tux. The biggest problem facing Bond 26 is the usual checklist of concerns that face any new James Bond film. Coming up with new stunts. Keeping up with the action movie rivals. Coming up with a vaguely topical plot. Keeping Bond relevant. Finding a good script. Casting good actors. Finding interesting new locations. Coming up with new gadgets. And making sure the marketing campaign and release date affords the film every advantage possible when it hits the cinemas. These will be the prime concerns of Bond 26 and any Bond film you care to mention. But choosing a new 007 is always fun for the fans and media alike. Long may the casting of James Bond continue. Let's hope that agent 007 really is forever.

ALSO BY THE SAME AUTHOR

**Timothy Dalton's James Bond –
The Retrospective**

-

No Time To Die – The Unofficial Companion